Portraits in Pastel

PORTRAITS IN PASTEL
by
LESLIE B. DeMILLE

"SIC ITUR AD ASTRA"

MVH PUBLISHING — CALIFORNIA

Paperback Edition

First Printing, 1981

First published 1981 in
the United States by MVH
Publishing, a division of MVH
International Enterprises, Inc.,
Post Office Box 2066
Costa Mesa, California 92626

Printed in the USA
by Frye & Smith
Costa Mesa, California

CONTENTS

LESLIE B. DeMILLE: AT A GLANCE

Leslie B. DeMille, a relative of the late motion picture producer Cecil B. DeMille, won his first prize in open competition at the age of eight years. Leslie was born in Hamilton, Canada, and attended the Art Student's League in New York. Later, he studied with the late artist and teacher Leon Franks in California. Leslie B. DeMille is many things to many people and organizations. He is an organizer, director, and instructor for portrait and still life affiliations throughout the United States, including Hawaii; and he is a juror for many major art shows across North America.

Leslie B. DeMille is a Fellow of the American Institute of Fine Arts in Los Angeles; a Fellow of the American Artists Professional League, Inc., in New York; a Past President of the Council of Traditional Artists Societies of California; and a Member of the Lahaina Art Society of Hawaii.

Following is a listing of exhibits, collections, awards, commissions, and publications:

EXHIBITS

Laguna Beach Festival of Arts 1965-1975
Death Valley '49ers, Inc.
        Annual Invitational Exhibit.................... Since 1968
American Artists Professional League
        Grand National, N.Y. .... Since 1971
Charles M. Russell
        Annual Auction of Western Art................. Since 1973

COLLECTIONS

Navy Combat Art Gallery, Washington, D.C.
Favell Museum of Western Art, Klamath Falls, Oregon
O'Brien's Art Emporium, Scottsdale, Arizona
Gallery Hawaii, Hyatt Regency, Maui

AWARDS

American Artist Professional League
        Best of Show, all media (Newington Award) 1971
        Gold Medal (Pastel).. 1976
        Margaret Dole Award...................................... 1979
        Wright Award... 1980
Best of Show, Catalina Festival of Arts 1972, 1974
Best of Show, San Gabriel Fine Arts 1972
Best of Show, Buena Park All City Festival 1973
Hors Concours, San Gabriel Fine Arts 1973
Best of Show (oils), Death Valley '49ers, Inc................... 1980

NOTED COMMISSIONS

NACAL Combat Artist (Navy Art) U.S. 6th Fleet,
    Barcelona, Spain.. 1972
NACAL Combat Artist (Navy Art)
    Pearl Harbor, Hawaii.. 1973
Annual Portraits of Past Presidents for Death Valley '49ers,
    Permanent Museum Collection
Joseph J. Gancie, V.P., ITT World Communications,
    Washington, D.C.
Portrait of former President Richard M. Nixon,
    Whittier College, California
Portraits of the four Past Presidents of Whittier College,
    California
Portrait of former Governor of California, Ronald Reagan
Portrait: Max Baer, Jr.
Portrait: Yvonne D'Carlo
Portrait: Andy Devine
Portrait: Buddy Ebsen

PUBLICATIONS

Who's Who in American Art
Dictionary of International Biographies
Who's Who in the West
Western Painting Today, Watson-Guptill, Publisher
How to Draw Cats and Kittens, Walter Foster, Publisher

L.B.D. ON L.B.D.

Pastel painting can be a very exciting medium with which to work. It's so versatile, for one thing. Things and effects can be achieved that virtually no other medium offers—the blending on the surface of one color over another, and the variations of these blends by subtle changes of pressure. These and a host of other results can be achieved immediately using pastels, whereas other mediums require much longer for the same effects— assuming they can be done at all.

In this book, as on my television show, I'll point out some specific areas to illustrate my points about pastels, so you can see for yourself what a rich field you can become a part of in art.

I've always thought that pastel lent itself to portraiture much better than some other medium usually thought of in connection with portrait painting. Maybe it's because of the soft, almost luminous quality that can be achieved through time and effort, and a little basic knowledge. For example, a child's face, or a rugged, craggy, colorful rogue can be done in a loose, impressionistic style. Yet both can yield visually convincing results, quicker and much, much easier with pastel.

Now don't get me wrong. I love oil painting very much, and I realize full well that there are things you can do with oils that cannot be done with pastel. But it works both ways, and what a wonderful change of pace to be able to work in one medium and then go right on to the other, feeling as confident in either.

Pastel painting is, of course, a discipline which translates itself to quickness. I don't mean to imply that speed is a requirement. Quite the contrary, in fact, if you want your finished work to reflect the care you have taken to capture your subject. When I say pastel is faster to work with, I mean it needs no drying time. And you can layer over your previous layers without hesitation.

The versatility of pastel is quite broad, especially if you expand your painting to include the many, varied surfaces available to you. I have purposely restricted the grounds used in the show and in the book to canson and velour paper. They are quite different from each other and, consequently, offer a wide variety of effects and experimental approaches.

There are, by the way, certain exponents of pastel who maintain that velour paper is unsuited for pastel painting. I disagree most adamantly, and include velour here. But you may draw your own conclusions from what you see in these demonstrations—and from how you fare when you try it out.

Remember one thing as you read this book, or watch my programs on television: my purpose in neither case is to show you how fast I can work with pastel, or to imply that one MUST work fast with it. My intent is to help you gain some basic knowledge about the medium and; through practice, develop your skill to the point where you are comfortable with pastels and yourself. That way, you can enjoy the fascinating results that can be realized with only a limited supply of colors, and my simplified approach to the world of pastel portraiture.

And one more thing: above all, enjoy.

Leslie B. DeMille

Leslie B. DeMille: a self-portrait

JUST WHAT IS PASTEL, ANYWAY?

Pastels are often confused with the harder chalk medium, where the pigment is mixed with oil or wax, and 18th century pastels have occasionally been listed as crayon drawings. Drawings made with colored chalk on colored paper and tinted with white, such as those of Fragonard (1732-1806), use techniques similar to those of pastel.

Pastels, however, are powdered pigments mixed with just enough gum or resin to bind them together. The word "pastel" itself is derived from the created paste, which is then moulded into the familiar sticks boxed by the manufacturer or put-up by the artist.

Pastel's immediate response, the charm and warmth of the delicate feel achieved by pure pigment on paper, is but part of the characteristics that distinguish pastels from oils. Pastel is a dry rather than a liquid medium. Therefore, pastel is technically the purest art medium since it uses the least binder and maximum, pure pigment. And since it is often the binder (not the pigment) that is the cause of deterioration in paintings—especially oil paintings—pastel is one of the most permanent art medium.

A BRIEF HISTORY OF THE MEDIUM

The history of pastel painting is relatively short. It wasn't until the 18th century in France that some of its earliest and finest exponents worked. One of the finest, a pioneer of the medium, was a Venetian woman, Rosalba Carriera (1674-1757). She was one of the few female artists to achieve fame before the 19th century.

She enjoyed tremendous popularity in France during the regency of Louis XV. And it was during this time that Quentin de la Tour (1704-1788), the greatest pastelist of his time, flourished. It was he who recorded the silks, satins, and opulent splendor of the rococo world, including the age of Madame de Pompadour, mistress of Louis XV.

Pastel painting became the vogue in France and by 1780, there were 2500 pastellists working in Paris alone. The freshness and spontaneity of the medium, combined with the Gallic craving for pomp and expression, were invigorating. And the best pastels of this period approached the spirit of French Impressionism, which wasn't to develop until a century later.

Degas, the most important pastellist among the Impressionists, collected the works of la Tour and developed the medium far beyond the accepted methods of the 18th century masters. Any artist who wishes to use pastel should study la Tour, Chardin, Degas, and the simplified but very effective techniques I have outlined in this book.

SOME GOOD ARGUMENTS FOR PASTELS

Pastel will allow you to paint in full color without the disadvantage of drying variations of color and speed, which you face in oils. It's also much easier than oil. Oil painting requires the basics of underpainting, glazing, the opacity and transparency of colors, and many other bits of knowledge. This, of course, doesn't mean that pastel painting requires less artistic ability. It merely requires less technical skill.

And if you're a comparative beginner, it can be a relief to work in a medium that frees you of some of the technical burdens. However, don't think that pastel is solely a medium for children. It may demand less technical skill, but it will call upon every artistic resource you can muster to create a meaningful portrait.

Portraits in pastel can be simple. You can start and stop when you want without worrying about colors drying when you want them to stay wet; waiting for colors to dry; squeezing paint out of a tube; selecting the right brush, medium, and knives.

Basically, pastel painting is a process of applying color directly to paper. No need to premix in a palette, since all mixing in pastel is done right on the paper. Simply apply the pastel to the paper, and the color you see is exactly the color you hold in your hand.

THE DeMILLE TECHNIQUE FOR PASTEL

There are three major techniques of pastel painting in use today. They are 1) Pointillism, 2) Impressionism, and 3) Painterly, or Layering.

What I call the DeMille technique is a combination of the last two — a simplified blend of impressionism and a layering of color, making maximum use of light to give the painting life.

If a comparison would help, my technique can be associated with glazing in oil painting, or possibly with washes in watercolor. That is, one layer of color over another without blending. This creates a rich buildup of flesh tones that have an almost sculptured, three-dimensionalism.

I think this is a fascinating method, and the results should motivate the casual painter as well as the serious pastellist. I know they still motivate me, or I wouldn't be using the technique today.

The DeMille technique is a strong and solid approach, which few, if any beginners even attempt without some kind of introduction. This is probably due to a misconception that pastels must be delicately laid down on paper, and cannot be stroked on with deliberate, controlled pressure, creating effects with a supple twist of the wrist.

Unfortunately, this prejudice is held by many writers on the subject who, for some unknown reason, fill their writings with such words as "fragile," "delicate," and so on.

Thousands of people have been trained this way, and truly believe that's the way one is to use pastels. But go to your library and museum. Look at the work of Degas. And you'll find his work anything but "delicate" or "fragile."

The DeMille technique will allow you to build successive coats of pastel until the desired effect is achieved. It will also teach you the point when to stop. And, as I'm fond of saying, "Knowing when to stop is as important as knowing where to start."

My technique also employs the color of the paper itself as a component of the painting, but not always as part of the painted area. The paper serves as the background area, or the area surrounding the color accent area.

The DeMille technique is quite beneficial to the beginner, because it reduces whatever feelings of intimidation you might have toward the medium. It actually encourages you to work in an aggressive, assertive manner on a structured shape, and helps you get rid of those lingering feelings of timidity.

I should tell you that it's quite natural for beginners in pastel to turn toward the rubbing method. With my technique, however, rubbing or blending is only done on the canson paper, and even then it is used sparingly. Instead, I will teach you the correct use of planes, angles, and values, all of those basics that seem to frustrate the beginner. In fact, my technique will give you insights into the craft of painting itself, and add to your ability in pastels or any other medium.

If you get tired or lose your inspiration, stop. Then later, when you feel the urge, begin again, without any elaborate preparations.

When you get right down to it, few things are as simple to begin and finish as a pastel painting. Just how simple it becomes will depend on how much you practice. Think of it as a way of art imitating life.

HOW TO START, AND WHAT YOU'LL NEED

If you're going to do anything correctly, you need the basic tools. And it's no different in pastel painting. So I'll list what you're going to need, and you can decide what you think you need, and what you think you can do without.

Easels   Easels come in every conceivable size and shape, from a $4.95 aluminum fold-up table model, to a $495.00 deluxe hardwood model with drawers and knobs. Buy what you can afford, and if you can't afford anything, improvise. If your desire to paint is strong enough, you'll devise something that will hold your paper flat and in a fixed position—somehow.

Stools   Any kind of painting should be relaxing. Sooner or later, you may want a stool. I prefer standing at the easel to allow me freedom of movement. The model will need something a bit more comfortable than a stool—something with arms, preferrably. After all, you're enjoying the artistic fulfillment, while they're just sitting there wondering what in the world you're going to make them look like.

Drawing Boards   There are a variety of models available, and the choice again is up to you. Because the paper you'll be using is very flexible and needs some support, you'll nccd something solid to draw on. However, I also use twelve sheets of plain paper over the board as a pad. Buy one at your local art supplier, or create something of your own.

Work Tables   Work tables are essentials. You need a place for your pastels, rags, fixative sprays, and the like. It's essential that you're comfortable as you work, so the table should be high enough so that you will not have to bend and stoop while reaching for your pastels. Once again, devise a system that works well for you. If you simply can't think of one, the salesman at your local art store will undoubtedly have all kinds of suggestions.

The Pastels Themselves   There is literally a bewildering array of pastel colors and hues out there from which to choose. For the sake of simplification, I have tried to make your initiation into pastel painting as painless as possible. From a range of 600 tints, I have personally selected 30 Rembrandt Pastels by Talens of Holland, for my personal technique in portraiture. I realize this might present a difficulty for those who already have a selection of pastels. But I also feel that the majority of you will benefit from this selection. I have, after all, devoted 45 years to the medium and the selection of my pastels, and they have rewarded me with many an art show prize.

In his *History of Color Painting*, Faber Birren lists the palettes of some famous artists throughout history. For example, Delacroix used 23 colors, Rembrandt just six. Each was a master colorist, and each had his own way to attain his artistic end.

There are no guarantees that if you use Delacroix's 23 colors, or Rembrandt's six, or my 30, that your paintings will equal theirs or mine in color proficiency.

However, taking advantage of my color selection, and watching my specific techniques on television and in this book, will give you a real advantage as you begin the rewarding pursuit of the perfect pastel rendering.

Paper   The pastel portraits that have survived from the 17th and 18th centuries are as fresh today as they were the day they were finished. And they were painted on paper. Paper is the easiest surface to obtain, and the least expensive for pastels.

There are many kinds of paper used for pastel painting. However, for our purpose here, I have selected a quality velour for ten of the portraits and, for the remaining three pictures, I have chosen Canson, from the French Canson Mi-Teintes line.

You can try as many kinds of papers and surfaces as you like for pastels but, for these portraits, we will use just the two I have indicated.

LET'S TRY SOME PASTEL

Painting with pastel should be precisely that — painting. To get the most out of the tools at your disposal, your pastel stick, and the most out of your finished painting, follow the basic structuring in each of the illustrations.

There are a multiplicity of methods used to apply pastel to paper. Most of them I have tried and eliminated in the formulation of my technique. And my technique is, once again, simply this: "Paint with your pastels, and make them serve your art."

Now, let's try some exercises.

To start, let's take a half stick of pastel. We'll use half so we can use it flat against the paper and better control it.

Now, start at the top of your paper and follow the example shown here until your strokes on the paper resemble those in the photograph. Use heavier strokes for more coverage. Use the heel of the stick when applying pressure and you get a hard edge. Ease up just a bit and let it fade to nothing. You can do the same with the head of the stick. Criss-cross your strokes, and you get a beautiful pattern.

Next, let's try a ball. Use a hexagon shape for the ball, rather than trying to draw a circle. Consider your light source. Following the example, put the shadow in the proper place. Also, to get the ball to sit down on the surface, you must place a shadow under it and coming away from it on the opposite side of the light source.

Now take your pale yellow, break it in half so it's a proper length, and use it the same way you did the darker color. Get the feel of the pastel. Learn how to get different textural effects by manipulation and control of the stick.

Following the example shown, lay in some color and then lay one color over the other. The shading and blending of color is the layering technique.

Now you have begun to truly paint with pastel. Continue to practice with the manipulation of the stick and the control for tone and effect, then complete the ball by adding the needed highlights. When you have completed one that is like the example shown, you have made the most important step towards portrait painting with pastel. Because, you see, structuring a ball is not that much different from structuring a face and head.

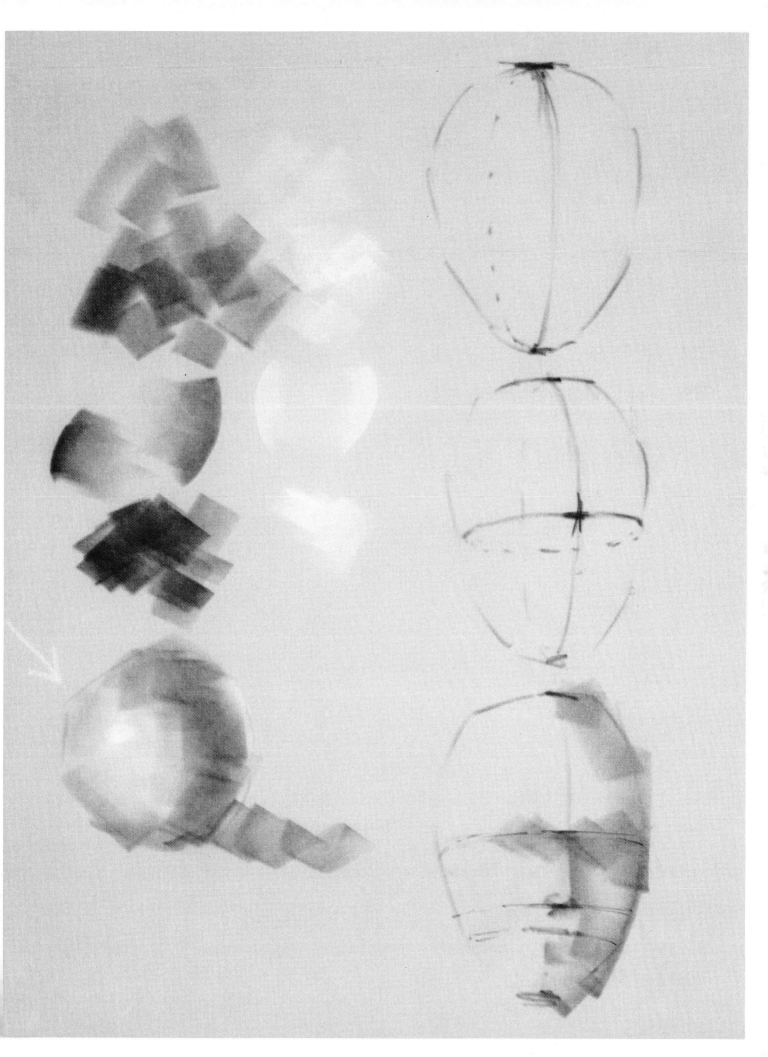

No amount of reading can replace the value of actual experimentation. Get to know your pastels, your paper, yourself. Practice, practice, practice. Then, when you think you've practiced enough, practice some more.

For the beginner, the most important thing is to begin. Take your basic tools and start. The sooner you do, the sooner you'll know what you really need. Forget the impulse, common among beginners, of trying to look like an artist. Let your work speak for you. Then, if you really are an artist, you'll look like one without ever having to try.

And now, let's go on to the portraits.

THE PORTRAITS

"THE ARTIST"　　　　　1981
Portrait of William (Bill) Alexander
26" x 20" velour paper
Rembrandt pastels

A face many will recognize, Bill Alexander. I have known Bill for many years, and it was a pleasure to have the opportunity to paint his portrait.

Note the soft color of his skin and the easily-recognizable character of his mouth and eyes. These were definite focal points of likeness to achieve. However, remember that the portrait is an interpretation, not a photographic reproduction.

I. STRUCTURING THE BASIC SHAPE

In this first portrait we'll learn some of the basics that are repeated throughout this book, and are an elemental part of the DeMille technique.

First, break your pastel to a manageable length, approximately 1 to 1½ inches. This will make it possible for you to handle the pastel with more control while working the color on the paper. Always work shadows away the line of definition by using the head or the toe of the stick.

Okay, let's start with our dark sanguine and structure the egg shape. That is, of course, the basic shape for all human heads.

Now, imagine there's a string around the egg from the top to the bottom. This is the center line, and will determine the angle that our subject is positioned in. Run the imaginary string around the egg so that you can see it continue up the back.

Now make a line that crosses the vertical line about halfway down the egg shape, and continue it around the egg as you did with the vertical line. Be careful to position this line exactly as you want your subject to appear to be looking.

The nose is placed in a similar manner at the halfway mark between the line for the eyes and the bottom of the egg shape. This line is especially important, because it also gives you the positioning for the ears.

The mouth placement is slightly above the halfway mark between the nose and the bottom of the egg shape. As always, run the string around the egg for a better perspective of the placement.

Now then, squint your eyes. Eliminate all the confusion of features and just concentrate on the lights and darks of the subject. You can begin to see the shadows and highlights, so let's lay in some shadows for the eyes, nose, and the side of the face.

II. HIGHLIGHTING

Take your pale yellow #227,9, squint, and look for the light source. For our subjects, we have positioned all the light coming from the same direction, left to right.

Once the light source has been determined, squint your eyes again so that you can see the light and dark patterns on your subject. Now, using this as your guide, lay in the highlights as you see them. Work the entire face. Don't be afraid to make a mistake. To paraphrase Alfred Lord Tennyson, "It is better to have tried and failed than never to have tried at all." (Apologies, Mr. Tennyson.)

However, in any attempt at art, you're always a winner, so lay in those highlights. Remember: squint, and eliminate all the in-between tones. Keep putting in the light patterns as you see them. Now you can begin to see the facial characteristics emerge. After all the highlights have been established, lay a thin layer of the pale yellow over the entire skin surface of your painting. Don't worry about covering your sketch, because it should now be permanently established.

III. THE FLESH TONES

This next step will add the beginning flesh tones to your painting. Take your light sanguine, and, laying it sideways against the painting, lay a thin layer over the entire face. Now you can see that this has given the painting a warm flesh tone base. Just look at the change that has taken place so quickly.

We still need more warmth, though, so use your red #371,5,

and softly blend it to the nose, cheeks, around the eyes, and on the lips. Don't forget the laugh lines and the ears. Now stand back and look at your painting. You'll notice that there seems to be too much red. So, to neutralize this effect, we'll use our gold ochre #234,7, and lay it over the cheeks, nose, chin, and in the areas furthest from the light source. The color now becomes more ochre, especially in the neck area.

IV. DETAILING

Now we'll use the dark blue #727,3 in the shadows.

Squint. Now lay it into the shadows lightly at first. Notice that I don't blend with my fingers. On velour, you don't blend that much, anyway. The upper lids of the eyes cast a cool shadow because the light is above them. Lay in the shadow up under the eyelids, the corners of the mouth, and into the shadows on the side of the face. Pull it into the hairline and shoulder. By the way, never use black in flesh tones. Why? It's just too black.

Now, take your dark sanguine and work it into the cool shadows. The dark sanguine allows you to draw more and, therefore, define the shadowed areas. (Remember: shadows are generally cool; and lights, warm.)

Shadows should always be simplified, while highlights should be more structured, and portray more detail.

V. A SKIN TONE SECRET

This next step is the one that most people find hard to accept until I help them to see it. The secret is GREEN. In most skin tones, there exists the color green. Squint, look closely at your subject, and separate the various colors that exist. Now look for the green hues.

With your soft olive green #620,7, gently blend the color

over the cool areas, and into the reflected light. As you can see, it really enhances the skin tones. It also helps turn the contour away from you.

Squint once again. Now your eye can detect a green hue in your subject's hair. Use a lighter green, #608,9, in the light flesh tones to achieve the same effect.

VI. EYES

In this particular portrait, we want to achieve the twinkle that Bill's eyes exude. And we want to accent that intense blue color.

First, take your black and enhance the shadow up under the lid. As always, refer to your light source, and you can see where the appropriate shadows will be needed. Now, with your light blue, #640,9, add color to the eyeball and to the iris. Work both eyes at the same time. Take your pale yellow and add that "sparkle" to his eyes. See? He's looking at you now.

VII. HIGHLIGHT DETAILS

While you still have the pale yellow in your hand, let's take another look at the highlights in the flesh tones. Controlling the pressure, lay in the highlights on the forehead, nose, cheek, and chin. Again, squint and just lay in the highlights that you see. Make sure that you are referencing the light source, too.

Let's take the raw umber #408,5 and add hair. Holding your pastel flat against the paper, pull the color into the skin while lessening the pressure as you approach the hair line. Don't over work the hair, either.

VIII. FINISHING TOUCHES

Go back over your portrait now. Check the highlights, shadows, and details. Take your white pastel and lay in his shirt. Just an indication is all you really need. Take the blue grey #727,7, and lay in his jacket. Just give the illusion. Don't attempt to make it too detailed, or you'll lose the impressionistic feel of the portrait. Now add some shadow to the shirt collar, and to his upper lip. There, I think you've got it.

As I'm fond of saying (just ask some of my friends), knowing when to stop is every bit as important as knowing where to start. So don't fidget with your painting. It's done. If you're not quite satisfied, that's perfectly natural. You'll do better with each effort you make.

You've just completed your first portrait. Look at it. See how much you've achieved in such a short time. Now don't wait to start your next portrait. Apply what you've learned on this one to your next effort as soon as you find a subject that you would like to paint. Oh, and try to make sure, also, that the subject doesn't mind being painted by you.

As you try each of the portraits in this book, or portraits of people you know, refer to each of the steps you have just completed. These steps are the basics for every portrait you will do.

"SUMMER SHADOWS"   1981
26" x 20" velour paper
Rembrandt pastels

Shadows on a model's face are sometimes avoided rather than used to take advantage of the subject. I have won awards because of the shadows and the way they are used in the portrait to add interest to an otherwise ordinary portrait. In this portrait, interest is added not only by the shadow, but also by the play of light created by the shadow.

"SUMMER SHADOWS"

I. STRUCTURING THE BASIC SHAPE

In the structuring of this portrait, we have to use our imagination to determine where the top of the egg shape will come, because of the hat. Study the portrait very carefully before you start, so that you can see the placement of the hat on the basic egg shape.

Now, let's take the dark sanguine and begin the basic shape. Follow each of the step-by-step photographs (pages 76-77), and don't go to the next until your drawing looks like the one represented in the photograph. Remember, it doesn't have to be exact, but close enough to build the next stage on top of it, and close enough to achieve the result that you're looking for.

Okay, let's structure the head. Under the hat, there's the egg shape which you have to imagine is there, continuing through the hat. The eyes about halfway down again. Now the nose, and the beautiful mouth. Next, the shadow. The shadows here will come right across the eye and the eyes themselves are going to be almost lost in the shadow. But this gives you the basic start. When you put the hat on, make sure it comes beyond the egg, so that it gives you enough width for the hat to be placed properly.

I want to draw the hat a little more carefully now. Make sure that you have the space here for the eyes where they would go if you could see them at all. And the rim of the hat — a nice, big hat — just let it keep on going. You see, it gives the effect of a summer day, and her being so happy and enjoying that summer sun will further enliven your portrait.

Draw the neck line, now. Again, the neck is a cylinder, so you have to make it look round with contour shadow. Her shoulder line comes down below the chin. Now your painting is beginning to emerge.

II. HIGHLIGHTING

It's very important to maintain, especially on something like this, the right positioning for the model. That's because these patterns of light do tend to change quickly if you don't keep the model in the same spot. With this in mind, lay in the patterns of light that filter through the hat. Just a suggestion, mind you, of where you want them to go. There's one down the side of the cheek. There's the suggestion of one over there on the shadow side, and then the nose emerges out of the shadow with a highlight on the tip. There is another on the cheek, although down under the lower side of the cheek so it's not as bright here as it would normally be higher on the cheek.

The nose casts a shadow just like the hat does, and it blends away. The mouth (squint your eyes now, and you can see where it should be) is dark red on the upper lip, and lighter on the lower. Now we have those shadows and highlights in.

III. THE FLESH TONES

Let's take our light sanguine color and, as before, run it right across the flesh tones to give instant color on the flesh. It's a summer day filled with sunshine, so she has quite a bit of warmth on her face so use your red #371,5 to add the warmth. The cheeks in these light areas that are coming through are especially warm, and the nose, of course, is quite warm — as are the lips. Even in the shadows, the cheeks are warm. I haven't even shown the eyes, you'll notice. I think we should give an indication of where they will be so that, even though they're just hinted at, they'll still be in their proper place.

So, suggest the eyes back in the shadow.

She has such a beautiful mouth, I want you to keep it soft and very loose in the beginning, so that any minor corrections that you need to make can be made without getting everything all muddied up. Use your dark red #318,5, just to add a little bit of that lucious color. Good. Is your painting beginning to emerge now? If not, follow each step until it does.

IV. DETAILING

Drawing is still the most important part of painting, even though the painting is "painted." And even though it is impressionistic, you still need the initial drawing to be correct if it's to turn out properly. So I want you to add something into the shadows. Not the deep blue or blue/grey that we sometimes use, but the soft blue/grey #727,9 which we will use instead. Because the shadows, being cool against the warm sunlight, will create a kind of special coloring. And this is what we're after — the soft cool tones that appear with the warm light.

At this point, let's indicate the hat. Because, after all, without the hat, we wouldn't have these shadows, and the pattern of light wouldn't happen. So we do have to indicate it now, using our pale yellow. And it's just an indication, nice, loose, and fresh. I can't overemphasize the idea of keeping it loose — impressionism is the word.

Now take the raw umber #408,5 and lay some of that under the brim just to indicate the hat coming around the forehead. When you squint, of course, the hair just disappears into the shadows, so let it disappear. And, even under the hat when you squint, you see a suggestion of the hair coming through. When it comes out into the light, that's when you start seeing some of the curls and texture appear on the hair.

So we just lay that umber in on the shadow side as well. Get the cheekbone to emerge. By squinting again, you can see that hair and cheek merge, so let it. Under the chin you can see where it kind of pulls together, and along the side there's a little sharp edge. Make use of the lost-and-found edges. It adds to the freshness of your portrait.

You should see the hair coming through now. And you can see the effects of tone you are getting, both warm and cool. We can use this same umber color to add little holes in the hat, and that gives us the effect that we'll need for the light coming through. Don't spend too much time here, just suggest. We have a nice ribbon around her hat. Use the dark blue/grey here, #727,3 and add the red violet tone #546,5 over that.

Remember where your light source is coming from. Now, add some more highlight to the lips to make them stand out. Use a little deeper red, the rich carmine red #318,5, on the shadow side of the lower lip.

Now, take the dark sanguine, and add in the little dark areas around the mouth to accent the lips and, at the same time, any detail you want to show on the rest of the facial features. Pull this color through the shadows as well, to help it merge even a little more into the portrait.

V. EYES
The dark blue in the eye area, and into the shadows as well, is quite deep. Squint real hard so that you can diffuse the eye as much as possible without having to detail it. Squint again. Match up the eyes as to their depth, size, and their position. Use a little bit of

highlight color to bring the hat out even more. Now for some more highlights. Put in the highlight on the nose to bring it forward. Work the eyes a bit more to indicate them in the shadow.

See? She's looking at you already.

VI. HIGHLIGHT DETAILS
Squint your eyes again. You can see where the light blends through on the right side and on the chin. The chin has to have a highlight to make it come forward where it's supposed to and not be so heavy down where the neckline is. We should give her some clothes about now, too. Just put in a little pink #546,8, again just a suggestion of clothing.

In the shadow, use the soft blue-grey #727,7 on the clothing as well. By using a soft blue, you see how that makes a nice effect of shadow. Sometimes we use a green to show the reflective light. Use the blue-grey #727,9, on the shadows of the reflective light. This adds coolness to the shaded areas.

I think you need some light in the hair with a gold ochre #234,7, just a suggestion of curls coming through. By using different pressures on your pastel, you can create different patterns and illusions, and even show a few little strands of hair by flipping the tip of your pastel in a circular motion over the hair area.

Now put that nice big earring in, with a shadow under it to make it stand out. Make it a soft, pink tone, just over the white, and add a highlight back onto it. Very pretty, don't you think? The upper lip should be just a little softer and deeper to accentuate the lines of her full lips.

Use a little dark sanguine with the ochre and umber and

green to bring out some warmth in her hair. There are more colors in the hair than you might think. Now work the hat again. Because of the light coming from the left side of the portrait, I think we need to suggest very softly a shadow on the right side of the crown.

Also, warm up this shadow a bit to make the hat look even warmer—notice the nice warmth to the straw. Just by blushing the light sanguine over the whole area, it warms it up to make it more than just pale yellow.

Now, go back and accentuate your shadows, and put in the stronger patterns of light. You have to put them in strongly to really make the portrait come alive. See? You can make shadows work for you—not against you.

VII. FINISHING TOUCHES
Now review your portrait. Check the shadows and the light in the shadows to make sure you've captured the focal point of the picture, which is the shadow. Look at the hat. Make sure the holes in the hat are there, and that the highlights on the straw give the hat the texture and sunny feeling we want to capture.

Satisfied? If not, go back over the painting. But remember once again, knowing when to stop is every bit as important as knowing where to start.

In this portrait, you've learned how to make shadows really work well. Try this painting a few times before going on to the next one. After all, you can never practice too much. But you can practice too little.

"THE SEA CAPTAIN"   1981
26" x 20" canson paper
Rembrandt pastels

*Do you remember Gregory Peck as Captain Ahab
in the great sea classic "Moby Dick"? Just the
thought of that picture creates visual images of the
sea for me, and for many others. For this portrait,
I'd like to share my "Sea Captain" with you.
It should be another good addition to your
portrait collection.*

"THE SEA CAPTAIN"

I. STRUCTURING THE BASIC SHAPE

In this portrait, we have a double problem to consider in structuring the basic shape. On one end of the egg shape we have a hat, set at a rakish angle. And on the other end, we have a beard covering the chinline. The problem is simply overcome by remembering the basic egg shape, and establishing the oval, as in every portrait we'll do. So let's draw the egg shape now, disregarding both hat and beard.

Next, locate the center line. Make sure, also, to continue it around the entire oval. The eyes are established by a line halfway down the oval, so put in the eye reference line.

The nose is halfway between the chin line and the eyeline. The mouth is slightly above the center line between the nose and the chin. However, it is covered with an impressive moustache, so just indicate the position, and we'll come back to it later.

As you've probably noticed, we're using canson paper in this portrait. The application of the pastel is a little different, and I'll explain the difference as we go along.

So let's refer to the step-by-step photographs (pages 78-79) in doing "The Sea Captain," and complete each step so that we have a reasonable likeness of the portrait you see in this book.

II. HIGHLIGHTING

Now put the highlights in. Squint, and see where the light areas are, and put them in with your pale yellow #227,9, in all the areas where they're needed. Squint again, and simplify these shadows or lights. Make it easier on yourself. When you squint, it really eliminates the middle tones that you don't want to be involved with just yet.

Indicate the light on the nose, and the part of the cheek that shows in the shadow. Now the light side of the cheek, and more highlighting in the eyes. There is even some flesh tone appearing down through the beard.

Don't forget the ear. The ear is something like a nose. They don't really do that much to your portrait, but just kind of hang there. However, they do make an important part of the portrait when it's done.

III. THE FLESH TONES

Lay in the light sanguine, and I mean lay it all over. See how it works differently on the canson paper. On the canson, you can smudge it in with your fingers and pull it together. Don't worry about the drawing —it will still be there.

Now we have some warmth in there that we didn't have before. Now take the pale yellow #227,9 and indicate the beard working it up into the face. Get the volume of the beard— lay it on, take a finger, and smear it on. At the same time, we can add a little bit of hair, just to indicate where it will be.

Now let's get some strength into the shadows. Use the dark blue/grey #727,3 and lay in the shadows. Where it comes against the nose, it should be soft. Indicate the nostrils. We'll get some depth into the eyes at the same time—just a little bit with the dark blue/grey. Pull it together by lightly smudging. Use some of the same color to indicate the hat line. It's a black hat, but indicate it with some of the blue and spread it around a bit.

Now we have to get a lot more color into his face. Take the red #371,5 and work it into the blue, working out of the shadows into the light with the red color. Now add the gold ochre color #234,7. See how raw the red looks without the ochre. So continue the ochre

where you think you need it. On the nose it will be a little redder, so don't use quite as much.

IV. DETAILING

Put some gold ochre #234,7 into the moustache area to give it a little more color. Now use the green tone #620,7 for the flesh in the shadow areas, and #608,9 on the light side. This will add believability to the flesh tone color. Add a little raw umber #408,5 to give more depth to the moustache and beard area. Squint, and let it fade away wherever you can.

Now add dark sanguine to the flesh tones over the blue/ grey to add definition. His coloring is deep, so use a dark color, #538,3, but just for the shadows.

Let's add some more depth to the hair on the side of his head with dark blue. Get some black in the cap, also. The black, if you squint, just forms the cap, around the forehead, and comes around close to his face.

He has a bluish T-shirt, so add a few little touches around there. Brighten up the highlights a little with the pale yellow color #227,9. Also lighten the cheek bone, and now lay in more hair that comes all the way through to the beard.

V. EYES

All right, now let's go to work on the eyes with black for depth. He has grey/blue eyes so let's show a grey/blue in the iris and in the white of the eye. Now put some highlights with #227,9 which will bring up the light on the face and the wrinkled brow to make him look as rugged as you can. Get some light on the cheek, too. Now you can see it coming out. Don't forget the light on the nose.

There is a shadow that his beard is casting, so add your

blue/grey #727.3 to it. Let it kind of blend together right into his clothing.

Now, a little more greenish tone on the side of his face might help turn it away at the side. There he is. You can almost smell the salt air. But he still needs some life in his eyes. So put it in and see what a difference it makes. Now he not only has life in his rugged skin and beard, he's got life in his eyes, too.

VI. FINISHING TOUCHES

Now review your portrait.

Have you captured the rugged, salty character that you wanted? Squint, and see if the highlights and shadows are accented just the way you want them. And last but not least, check the light in his eyes. This one little detail can mean the difference between a dull portrait and an exciting one.

Practice this portrait a few times before going to the next one. The photo references will add to your ability to achieve effects that would otherwise take you much longer. Visual association is the most important tool we can use in learning our craft.

So read the book, watch my show on television, and you'll be amazed at the progress you will achieve in a much shorter time than you think.

This illustration shows the basic structure for this portrait.

"SPRING WATER"   1981

26"x 20" velour paper
Rembrandt pastels

*For years, artists have tried to catch the essence of
the American Indian. We'll try to do that, too, and try
to capture the essence and beauty that is eternal
as spring water. In fact, Spring Water is this Indian
child's name, who is half Navajo and half Apache.
So in this portrait, we want to capture the look of
the past, and blend it with the hope of the future.*

I. STRUCTURING THE BASIC SHAPE

Softly at first, put down your egg shape, and get it positioned where you want it on the paper. Her eyes are centered between the skull and the chin. Her head is tilted forward a little bit, too, as you'll notice. The nose line is positioned halfway down the egg, and the mouth is above halfway in between the nose and the chin.

Make sure you give her enough volume for her head. You see, she has her head turned almost to a ¾ profile. That means the back of the head will begin to show more, and you have to make sure you get enough of it back there.

Now indicate the hair and her beautiful tie in the back, typical of the Navajo we're trying to capture. The ear is on the same line as the nose and the eye. Half of the ear is hidden.

Notice how far back the neck appears, and the line of the blouse comes just above the chin line and then down. These are important areas. If you get them too high or too low, you have either someone with a long neck, or someone with no neck at all.

Now we can work with the mouth. The upper lip is shaded, and the lower lip catches the light. Put more dark under the lip. Squint your eyes, and look at the shadow on the nose. You don't have to outline it. All you need is the shadow on the side. When you put the highlight in on the other side, you've got it.

Now the eyes. Make sure you get them lined up, one with the other. At this time, just indicate the upper lid part and let the color blend into the iris — but just an indication for right now.

II. HIGHLIGHTING

Highlight the flesh tones with #227,9. Squint, see where they fall and add the highlights where you need them. The lower lip is a plane of light, and runs into the flesh tone as well as the cheek.

III. THE FLESH TONES

Take the light sanguine and lay it on as you have in the past. Don't be afraid to give it lots of color. This is the same light sanguine color that we have used for the other portraits. When we use the stronger red color, we'll get a deeper tone, sort of coppery, to give us the beautiful Indian complexion we're after.

Now take your red #371,5, and lay in some warm color. Squint. This will help you see where the warm spots are. Around the eyes, there should be warmth, and the ear, of course, is always warm.

With the same red, lay in the blouse. Now you can see that you need some *more* red in the flesh tones. Don't fall short in the flesh tones. Now, use the gold ochre #234,7, and lay it on softly, letting some of the red bleed through.

At this time you should show some shadow tones in her face. So, very softly, use the dark blue/grey #727,3 to lay in some shadows. Go very carefully so you don't overdo it. Remember: on the velour, don't smudge with your finger. Just lay one color over the other.

Keep the mouth itself warm, trying not to use too much blue. Lay in the forehead line, indicate the hair, and very quickly, lay in the body of the hair. Let the hair merge with the flesh wherever you can. Keep it loose and free form.

IV. DETAILING

Now take the dark sanguine to finish up the shadow tones, to kind of pull together where you have the dark blue for the shadows. Use it under the nose for a little bit of shade, and use it on the lips a little. Keep the lips soft, of course. You can use this sanguine color for the shadow of the blouse but just an indication.

Next, put some light back into her face. Not too much, because her complexion is very dark. Indicate the highlight on the nose. See how that brings the nose forward, just like the cheek? Put some light on the lower lid of the eye, too, because the lower lid catches the light.

V. EYES

Now we'd better give her some depth in her eyes.

Use the black for those big pools of darkness. Make them extremely dark and, where the upper lid comes over, let it cast the shadow into the eyeball as it's supposed to. The upper lashes you can just indicate. The eyebrows can be put in very softly first with blue/grey and then a touch of black.

Now let's add life into the eyes. Use a very soft touch of white here. Punch a little highlight in the first eye, then in the second to make them match. Now her eyes should start to focus on you.

VI. HIGHLIGHT DETAILS

Now put in some shadow that is cast by the hair, where it touches the cheek. Use a little more black to finish up under her ear. Use a little blue in the hair, a lighter blue/grey #727,7 just to bring out some of the light.

Now lay in the yarn hair tie with white. For the grey tones in the yarn, use your olive green #620,7. Next take the pale yellow #227,9 and lay it in over the shadows of the yarn to soften them. Let's also indicate the turquoise at this time with the blue #640,9. Add the shadows with dark blue and highlight with white, remembering the direction of the light source.

Now for some green tone on

the lighter side of the face. Use #608,9 on that edge to help turn the contour away from you. Put some under the nose, also.

VII. FINISHING TOUCHES
Now go over your portrait. Check it for the highlights. Are they all indicated the way you want them to be? Have you captured the innocent Indian maiden portrayed in the book?

Make sure you can easily spot the traditional turquoise against the red-orange Navajo blouse—make sure the play of color frames her delicate features the way they should.

You should be about finished with your portrait. Add a little warmth to the hair, so that it's softer, as befitting Spring Water. At this point you may start asking, 'Am I finished?' That's a difficult question to answer, and only you can do it. But remember, always leave something for the imagination. And, again, knowing when to stop is every bit as important as knowing where to start.

Practice will help you know both those things.

This illustration shows the basic structure for this portrait.

"THE COWBOY"   1981
26"x 20" velour paper
Rembrandt pastels

The American cowboy has always been a very interesting subject for artists. With the resurgence and popularity of Western art, I looked all over for a special subject, one that is reminiscent of the old west. And I knew just the person—Buster Stovall. It was also very convenient, because Buster is my friend. Always look to your friends for your best portrait subjects.

In this portrait, we want to emphasize the rugged features of the skin tones, and we want to establish the western feel of the painting with suggestions of the cowboy hat and kerchief.

"THE COWBOY"

I. STRUCTURING THE BASIC SHAPE

Put in your basic egg shape under the hat (just pretend the hat isn't there). Tilt the egg forward a little at the chin. Put the center of the eyes in now, which is down low because the head is tilted forward.

Next, the nose is halfway between the eyes and the chin. The mouth is above halfway between that—keep that in mind. Now the hat is sitting high up on the forehead. Make it nice and big so it doesn't look too small on his head. Always remember to make the hat bigger, so it won't look like a pill sitting on your subject's head.

Now position the ears on the line of the eyes and the line of the nose. The crown of the hat follows the line of the head—so you've got to give him space to put his head underneath. The kerchief, of course, comes along the shoulder line.

All right, now we can start tightening it up a bit by indicating the nose. He's a rugged old cowboy, so he's got to have strong features—don't baby the structure of the face.

Indicate the eye position remembering there's normally a space of an eye between the eyes. Also indicate the hairline a little bit. There's a nice shadow cast by those little wisps of hair coming across his forehead.

II. HIGHLIGHTING

Let's start laying in some lights about now. The light on his forehead should come first. Squint your eyes, and simplify those lights. Indicate the lights strongly, including the eyebrows, using your pale yellow #227,9.

On the lower lid, there's a catch of light. Put that in. Indicate the white of the hair, just a little bit. Okay, it's time to add some flesh tones.

III. THE FLESH TONES

Take your light sanguine, and go over the whole thing. There, he's warmed up a bit, and doesn't look like a ghost anymore. Now using your red #371,5, warm up the cheeks, mouth, and ears. The gold ochre #234,7 now goes over the red. You see how this changes more to a golden-red, almost like a flesh tone—which, of course, is what we're after.

Now, for some real depth, we take our dark blue/grey #727,3. Work with it very softly, and just lay it in the shadows a little bit. Indicate the eyes with this and, wherever you see shadowed areas, put it in there, as well. Not too much on the mouth, though. The mouth is usually softer. Don't forget underneath the mouth, as well as under the chin.

Now take a dark sanguine and go over the dark blue. This will give you a more natural shadow appearance. Keep the shadows simple and cool.

IV. DETAILING

Now let's put a hat on our subject. Take raw umber #408,5 and put in some hat shadows, keeping it loose. Just an indication is all you need. Lay in the contrast around the ear and the back of the hat. Some of this raw umber will also be good for the shadows on his hair. Not so much for the flesh tones, but mostly for the hair and, of course, the hat. Use gold ochre #234,7 for the light part of the hat.

Use a dark red #318,5 for the kerchief now because it'll have an effect on the flesh tones around it. Take a lighter red #371,5 now and go over it. Just get the general feeling of it.

Indicate the black on the vest next. A dark blue #727,3 is all that's necessary to show the deep shadow under the kerchief. Now a little touch of blue #640,9 to show the high- lights on the vest. Use your black over these colors to give the extra depth it needs. Now, for the shirt, use any color you want. You're the artist, and you can do it any way you wish.

V. HIGHLIGHT DETAILS

Go back to the flesh now and indicate some highlights with #227,9. Lay in some of the lighter tones, put in some of the wrinkled brow using the lighter sanguine, not the dark. Put some light in the nose, keeping in mind where your light is coming from.

Now use a little black around the eyes to get more depth.

Start indicating the hair. Use the gold ochre in the hairline, to give the grey hair some color. It isn't just all white, you know.

Give some color to the moustache, too. Now, take the white and indicate the eyebrows.

VI. EYES

I think we should now put a little bit of a light in his eyes. If you want to give him a little bit of a twinkle, do so by putting some light right above the lower lid on his eyeballs.

Show the lower lid again on the eye, with the indication of light that hits there. On the shadow side, it's just a slight indication. Work the eyes until you have achieved the look you want.

VII. FINISHING TOUCHES

Make him a little more rugged now. He *is* an aging cowboy, after all. Accent a little more here and there with lights and darks to strengthen his character. And remember the shadows.

Use some pale yellow for the moustache, and go over it with a pure white, to add dimension.

Now look at your painting. Could he use a little more light on the ear, or a little more color? Or does he need a little more warmth on his face and nose?

Remember he has nice warm cheeks. If that looks good to you, I'm going to tell you to stop.

I won't always do that, and most of the time, you'll have to decide for yourself when to stop. But, for this portrait, let's call it quits. Practice this portrait before you go on to the next. And try for that ruggedness that typifies the Old West. Achieve that, and you've achieved "The Cowboy."

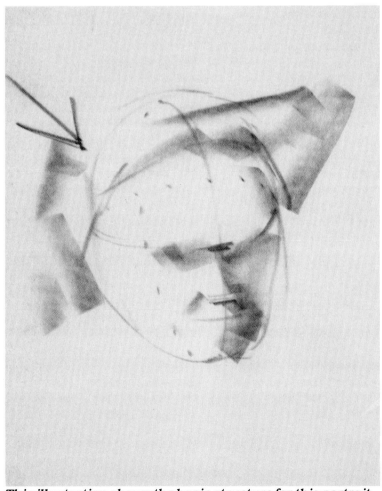

This illustration shows the basic structure for this portrait.

"NATIVE SON"   1981
26" x 20" velour paper
Rembrandt pastels

In this portrait, we have a subject that has always fascinated me. For years I have painted the American Indian, but I could never begin to exhaust the endless variety of subject matter. This model is very special. He is a Chippawa, father of Spring Water, another model in our portrait series.

In this painting, we will portray the pride of the past and the determination of the future. And we'll capture the strength of his features, especially the strong nose.

"NATIVE SON"

I. STRUCTURING THE BASIC SHAPE

In this portrait, I have positioned our native son in this particular pose to achieve that determined look we're after. So let's lay in the basics for the painting.

Show the semi-profile with the egg shape. He's got his head tilted forward slightly, so the eyes are down below the level where they would normally be, and they extend upward. Now, lay in eyes, nose, and the mouth as you have in previous portraits.

Remember we want to show a lot of strength, and a lot of determination, so use a little "gusto"—a little more strength in the application. Squint to see the shadows, and lay them in. Next, draw the hairline and the shoulder line that comes up quite high.

Now where should the ear fall? We have the line for the eyes, and the line for the nose parallels that. Therefore, the ear has to fall between those two lines. Then, the hair comes across. Next, the jawline juts forward. Then there's that beautiful hair tie, which adds so much to the whole portrait.

Get the shape of the head in. Indicate the neckpiece that he's wearing—another traditional part of his dress.

We have to establish the features a little more now, so put in the determined mouth. Use the heel of the pastel as I've shown you in the past to create some of those lines. Now the nose has to be structured carefully, and the brow as well, to capture the concentration that he's showing. Make sure your proportions are fairly correct before you continue with your color.

II. HIGHLIGHTING

Now put in your highlights, showing the little wrinkle in the brow. Put highlights on the nose and all those other areas that the light will be hitting. Don't forget the high cheekbone. The upper lip has a crisp outline and the lower lip has a play of light on it, going around into the shadow. Give an indication of the lower lid to show strength.

Okay, don't forget to put some kind of detail in the ear, but keep it simple, suggestive.

Now let's lay in some color.

III. THE FLESH TONES

Use the light sanguine color to lay over the top of what we have done and give him some immediate color. Carry the flesh tone up into the hair area, and now strengthen it with some of the red #371,5

The ears, of course, are always warm. On the shadow side, get the strength of shadow and warmth in there, too. Because, when we use this amount of red, it will allow us to apply more of the gold ochre #234,7 over the red, as we've done in the past.

Just softly glaze over with the red #371,5 now. You can see the flesh tone coming through nicely. And by adding the gold ochre over that, and just a little back in the shadow, the tones emerge even more.

And, speaking of shadows, now we have to get to them.

IV. DETAILING

Lay in a little gold ochre in the shadow areas. Keep it subtle, and indicate the eyes, soft and determined. I don't usually use the dark blue/grey #727,3 in the lips, but he has such strength in them that just a little indication to give them added determination won't hurt. Lay some in on the jaw, underneath the jaw and, of course, down where the shadow is created by the jewelry he's wearing.

Let the hair run right into the flesh tone using the blue/grey. Squint your eyes, and see how it merges. Now, show the vest, his hair tie, and the braids in his hair. Use the light yellow color that we employ in our highlights. This can also be used to indicate the feathers.

I think we'd better strengthen his features with the dark sanguine, especially around the eyes, nose, and mouth. The dark sanguine helps to strengthen the mouth and lose some of the dark blue that is so obvious. And, again, use the greenish tone that enhances the flesh so much. All right, we've got our basic color.

V. EYES (and more detailing)

Now we need more depth into the eyes. Use the black, retaining that determined look.

Don't use the black on the flesh tones. It tends to dirty the flesh color. Use your dark blue and your reds and umbers and the dark sanguine mainly. Now, let's add the highlights in his face, without losing the depth of the color underneath it. Pulling out the light here and there on his furrows will tend to add even more strength.

Again with the highlight, bring out the high cheek bone. Suggestion is the big thing to be thinking about. Don't get caught up in too many details you could do without. Get the mouth and the lower lip to look determined. This gives us the look we're after.

Now darken the hair where you think you need it with black. Bring a few hairs over the underneath tones, letting them merge with the flesh, and you've got the hairline. Strengthen the eyebrow a little, and come down behind his ear with the heel of the black to outline that ear and strengthen the hairline behind it.

Now indicate his braided hair, indicative of his tribal custom. By adding a tuft of hair at the bottom, it looks more real. Bring out the feathers now.

Put the black behind the feathers and crispen up the edge.

VI. FINISHING TOUCHES

Pull his hairline down. And put a little more indication in the hair ties with a little bit of black and some red beads that show. Also put a little tone in the feather for a bit more color. Take your finger and kind of grade the color down a touch in the feathers. Then take some pure white and pull that over it, to give a more feathery look.

The hair tie has beautiful colors, don't forget. There's turquoise, blue, pink — so add a little bit of each. Put some depth under it for a shadow, and then add a white catch light to make that edge come out.

While we're at it, use the light yellow color #227,9 to indicate the neck piece he's wearing. By doing this and adding a little bit of shading under it, it does indicate that he's wearing a necklace.

Indicate a little more light in the hair with light blue/greys.

Now, we're approaching the point of a finished portrait.

I think he could stand a little bit of light in his eyes. Just a kind of catch light on the lower part — for that determination and strength we're after. The nose, again, should be detailed a bit so it's more structured. Highlight the mouth.

Now we're just about at the point to say "Let's stop." Look at your portrait. Is the strength there? Can you see determination in the face?

Go back and indicate any highlights you think might need additional touches. Work on your shadows a bit. There, now it's really time to stop.

See you next portrait.

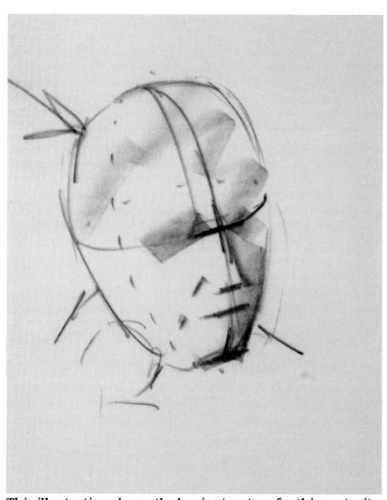

This illustration shows the basic structure for this portrait.

"INNOCENCE IN PROFILE"   1981
26"x 20" velour paper
Rembrandt pastels

In this portrait we have a subject thought by some to be difficult, and by others to be relatively easy. Both are correct. A profile is difficult because the drawing is a bit harder. It's easier in a way, though, because you've only got half the features to depict.
     This subject is quite beautiful in profile. Of course, I'm a bit biased, because the subject is my granddaughter, Marie.

"INNOCENCE IN PROFILE"

I. STRUCTURING THE BASIC SHAPE

First, let me show you the difference in structuring the profile. We start with the basic egg shape, but we have a difference this time: we extend the back of the egg to show the back of the skull. The center string in this profile is the outside line of the egg, going all the way around. The eyes still come halfway down. Then put in the nose and the mouth, using the guidelines we always use. The sideview of the eye is indicated, then the eyebrow goes in, and then the mouth.

Be sure to get the ear back far enough. Squint. One of the most common mistakes is not getting the ear back far enough on a profile.

Now indicate the hair over the skull line. Make sure you get enough depth in back where the skull contour goes. Squint and place the eye in just lightly, then lightly place the nose and mouth and chin. Can you see what I mean about there being more drawing involved in a profile than there is in other portraits?

Now refine that little upturned nose and the mouth as well, keeping it in position. Watch the line of the profile. Correct it if you have to before going on. The lower lip juts out a little bit, then comes back in. Shadow the brow that comes across the bone structure above the eye socket, and then the eye. Set it back far enough — don't get it too close to the bridge of the nose.

Now indicate the ribbon and that beautiful fall of hair coming back in behind. The ribbon we'll just kind of let fall away to nowhere. Show the ruffled dress very simply, with the strand of ribbon coming out the front and showing the shoulder line.

You will spend a little more time structuring this drawing,

as you can see. It's exceedingly important. Now let's lay in some highlights.

II. HIGHLIGHTING

We'll use our pale yellow #227,9. Indicate some on that upper lid, and upturned nose. Lay in some highlight on the cheek, and next to the cast shadow on the neck — and the portrait is starting to emerge now. Next: some color.

III. THE FLESH TONES

Let's lay in some color for the hair, doing it very, very loose and suggestive, again. Get the hair falling down behind her head. Now take the light sanguine and apply it to the flesh areas, to give her an overall warmth. See how warm the ear should be. You can see it even better if you squint.

Run this flesh tone into the hair and the eyes. Her complexion is a lot softer, a lot more delicate than some of the others we've done, so you don't have to use quite as much pressure to achieve the flesh tones.

There will be very little of the dark blue/grey #727,3 used for shadow. Put a little behind the ear to throw it forward of the shadow. The eye itself, of course, will have a little depth, and the pupil and iris will be in profile, too. Therefore, it's not a round ball, but an elliptical shape when seen from the side.

Add a little bit of depth in the hair now. Use the olive green #620,5 in the shadow of the hair. The hair is greenish now. There's a lot of green in blond hair, after all. Leave a clear area for the ribbon — we'll get to it later.

Now the flesh tone again. Use your red as in the past, then use the gold ochre to put over the reddish tone. Very softly blush the ochre over the red to make it a delicate flesh-like red-ochre tone, especially on the neck. The ear is warm enough

without the ochre, however. You can use the ochre in the hair, too, to give it warmth and change the color a little bit. There, the profile should be emerging even more.

IV. DETAILNG

Now we'll do that soft, delicate flesh. Use a light bluish grey #727,9. Apply it to the shadow portions beneath the mouth, softly. Now use some green value #608,9 on the flesh. Very softly blend it in along the side of the face. Some of the green into the hair at this time would be all right, too.

Now use the dark sanguine. Use it softly under the nose. The idea is, after all, to keep it soft and delicate. Suggest the upper lip. You can put the darker tones and warm tones in now.

Let's get the lights on the face, to add the contour. There's a little catch of light on that lower lid, a little catch on the upper also. By blushing #227,9 over the others, it gives the delicate skin tones we're after. Put some light on the chin and the lower lip, while you're at it.

V. EYES (and more detailing)

Now put a little light in the eye. You can see where the light should go. Now, the black — just a touch of it into the eye, up under the lid. Put some under where it's in shadow, and indicate the upper part of the iris and pupil. Indicate a few little lashes. Now a little white to brighten up the eye.

Use a very, very soft and subtle touch of umber #408,5 for the brow. And with this same umber, carry through now to bring the hair shadows back around for just a suggestion of hair. Her hair can be nice and sketchy here. Let it come down in the back. All of the soft tones play up the delicacy of her features, and the whole idea of this portrait is the model's youth, subtlety, and softness.

Use a little pink #546,8 for the dress. Suggest the collar, and suggest the shoulder line. With the pale yellow, you can even suggest the little bib area that comes around the dress, and accent some of the light on the pink. Use the darker red #318,5 for the red ribbon. Make it turn sideways, in profile, just as your model is. Add just a touch of red to the ribbon behind her hair, that's showing through. Lay in some light red #371,5 now for the lights. You can see how easy the ribbon is to do—and how believable it looks.

VI. HIGHLIGHT DETAILS

Now look at her ear— does it need some light on it? Keep it warm, of course, always warm, but the highlights are necessary. Show the jawline that comes up under the ear a little bit.

Getting back to the hair again, put some more of the gold ochre tone in. Get the volume of the hair first. We haven't used the yellow #201,5 very much, but put some in now. You can see how strong it is. When you think of blond hair you think of yellow, but *just* yellow doesn't look quite natural. So let's add a little light sanguine again, over the yellow, to warm it up. Then some light green. See the colors you can get. Squint, and look at all the colors in real hair. They're there if you really look for them.

Do we need a little shadow? Remember where your light is coming from. If you do, these back areas will be thrust into shadow using #408,5 umber, making the portrait even more realistic. Add a touch to her eyebrows, too. The real dark shadows are #727,3. Also, she has a cute little earring you should put in now. Use the red. Then, with the dark sanguine, put in the little shadow created

by the earring. For the highlight, use the pale yellow, or even white. And there you have an earring sitting there—what could be simpler?

VII. FINISHING TOUCHES

Now, the background. Use your blue/grey #727,7, and with the heel of the pastel, very carefully, cut right into the profile, and then come away from it into the background so the strokes don't show. Throw a little bit in behind the head, too, add some warmth with your dark sanguine, and you're getting close.

But before you stop, add one more touch to the ear, for highlighting—and you've completed the portrait. You see, it really was easy, wasn't it? But remember: the only way you'll ever find out just how easy, is by doing it for yourself.

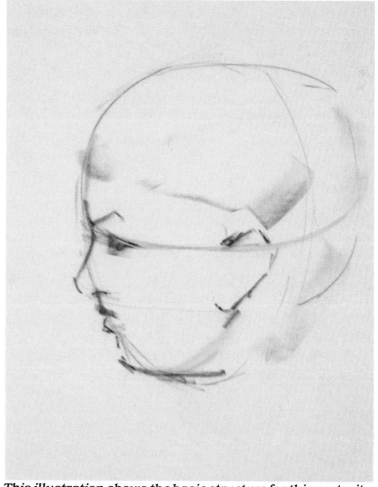

This illustration shows the basic structure for this portrait.

"RED" 1981
26"x 20" velour paper
Rembrandt pastels

Red hair and freckles, has to be one of the great all-American looks. And no portrait collection would be complete without at least one. To paint red hair, you must see all the colors that come together to create red hair. I'm going to show you how to do that with this portrait.

"RED"

I. STRUCTURING THE BASIC SHAPE

First put down your egg shape. Then the string, with the eyes coming through the center, along with the nose, mouth, and the shadow you'll see by squinting. Then the line of hair that comes across the face.

Next, the positioning of the ear. Follow the line of the nose and the line of the eye, as in previous portraits.

Now put in the neckline, and there's your structure. Structuring may seem repetitive, I know. But it's really the single most important guide that I, or anyone else, can give you.

Now let's establish where the hair is going to be on the egg. The egg comes under the hairline as if there wasn't any there. The head is tilted just a bit, you'll notice. Lay the eyes in, in relation to the center line. And lay in the shadows by squinting and seeing the shadows where they appear. Light pattern against shadow pattern is what you're after here.

You can see the jawline that pulls right down into the neck, the neck being, of course, a cylinder. Now indicate the loose, simple T-shirt that's so symbolic of a young boy. Refine the mouth a little now. The mouth is very soft and simple. It's not nearly as severe as you might think by looking at it all by itself.

Squint, and see how those shadows appear from the eyebrow and along the side of the face. His head is tilted forward slightly, throwing the ear up in the air a little more, so the ear comes up and disappears into his hair. The ear on the other side, naturally, will be in the same position. And what else would a red-headed boy have but two nice ears sticking out like that?

II. HIGHLIGHTING

Now put in the highlights with the pale yellow #227,9, and indicate the light area of the face. Keep the shadow on the side of the face and lay in your highlight. See how the lower part of the mouth shows the light, the contour. Underneath the lip, there's a shadow, as well as a puckered look on the chin.

The neckline is lost into the jaw, going right into the neck. Put a little pattern on the ear. That's what we're looking at — pattern rather than individual features. Remember: a likeness doesn't necessarily come from little details. So keep in mind that it's not the detail that always makes a likeness — it's a pattern and the impression that pattern makes.

Now for some color.

III. THE FLESH TONES

Lay in some color on his face, and, again, just lay it on there, using your light sanguine. Put it all over in the strength that you see in the portrait. Run this color all the way through his hairline. That gives us a basis for the hair already.

Now, take your dark blue/grey and put the shadows in the face and, coupled with the light that we have, it shows an intense shadow. Accentuate the broad nose and the eyes coming out of the shadow.

Squint. Don't try to pick out the jawline too distinctly, but you'll see there's a little accent under there, along with a shadow, that disappears into the neck. Now add some red #371,5 to the face, starting with the ear, and working across the cheeks. You may need more red there so you can add more of the ochre tone to lend it that golden color hue. Now put red on the lips, very softly. Then some red in the shadow in the ear, as well. This kind of red isn't really necessary in the hair, but a little won't hurt. As I said before, it takes a variety of color to make up red hair.

Now the gold ochre #234,7 is applied to the face. Softly blend this over the red tones, and you get a beautiful flesh tone. Use some on the neck, too.

Now I think we need some depth in the hair.

IV. DETAILING

Your dark burnt sienna #411,5 is more appropriate for the coloring in the hair. It's very red but, after all, that's the name of the painting. It won't remain all red, though, because there is green in blonde hair and red hair, as well.

So first the #411,5. Put that all over and show a little bit of the hair coming through and around his ear. Then use your olive green #620,5, to create the dark tones first.

Take a brighter green #620,7 and use it softly over some of the red tones. It kind of gives another color altogether and makes his hair coloring more believable.

Now put some gold ochre tones into the hair and blend it across. All of this gives the basis for the hair color. Use the dark sanguine to work the shadows in the face a little more. Use a little bit of shadow down the side of the nose. The lights will come in on the other side — always keep that in mind. Always reference your light source.

The ear that's in shadow should be toned down. Keep the mouth very, very simple. Under the ear, punch up the shadow a little bit on the hair to bring that ear forward. Your portrait is once again beginning to emerge.

V. EYES (and more detailing)

Now put some black into the eyes to strengthen them, and to add more depth. Work the dark up under the upper lids. Keep the depth up under where the light is hitting on the upper lid and casting that shadow underneath, making it very intense. Don't use your black anywhere else on the flesh tones.

Use your blue #640,7 for his T-shirt. Again, just an indication of the shirt, using the dark blue/grey for the shadow you see. Indicate that shadow that's cast and disappears around on the side.

Now you can add some light with the pale yellow back into the hair. And we can use it on the highlights of the flesh to bring out not only the flesh tones, but the form as well. Bring out the nose, too, and the youthful look comes through.

Indicate the eyebrows next. The lower lid of the eye, you remember, catches the light. Put a little bit of light into the eye to indicate the white. Remember that the eye is a ball. Show a little bit of blue in his eyes, too, to go with his shirt. Use it mostly on the lower part, his upper portion being deeper into shadow.

VI. HIGHLIGHT DETAILS
Now it's time to move over into the hair. Take the umber #408,5 and work that down into the shadows a little more, keeping the shadows a little simpler. Now put back a little more of the burnt sienna into the hair, to keep that red color.

Now on the light side, indicate that wavy curl coming through by putting a shadow underneath the curl. Take some white and get a little white into his eyes to brighten them up a little bit, too. That should add more of a "sparkle" to the eyes.

Now, let's pull together the colors in the hair by using the gold ochre. Lightly brush over the green, blue, ochre, burnt sienna, yellow, and off-whites. Add a little bit of gold ochre, also, into the eyebrows. They're not just white, they are a kind of ochre tone. We're getting

there, aren't we?

Add a little bit more gold ochre to the hair, to give him that "reckless" all-American boy look, but keep the loose feeling, at the same time. Now one more highlight on his face on the light side, and voila!

VII. FINISHING TOUCHES
Well, isn't that the great American look now? But I know what you're thinking. We forgot the freckles. So let's put those in right now—just lay them right in there.

The gold ochre may not be dark enough, so take your sanguine and lightly put in the freckles. Don't make them all the same size or intensity, but mix them up—like real freckles are. Some of them are soft. When they're over a highlight, soften them a bit, but show

their strength. Some light, some not so light, some dark.

And there you have it. The red-headed All-American boy. And that's probably the only time you'll ever see him that still.

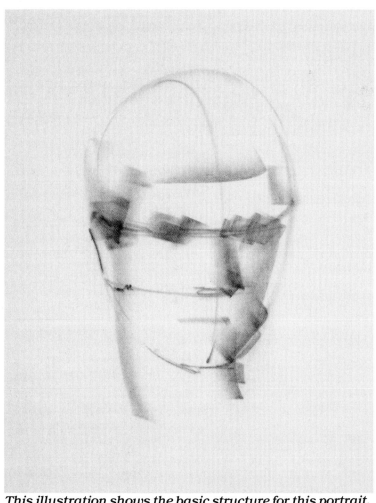

This illustration shows the basic structure for this portrait.

"GOLDEN EARRINGS" 1981

26"x 20" canson paper
Rembrandt pastels

This portrait displays an aspect of portrait painting this is totally different than all the others in our series. It is probably the one aspect that I'm asked more questions about than any other. And the most expected answer is not correct. I'll reveal the question and the answer to you as you're doing the portrait.

"GOLDEN EARRINGS"

I. STRUCTURING THE BASIC SHAPE

First off, we've got to give our model enough space for all that beautiful hair. Under that hair you have to visualize your basic egg shape. Get the center line with the string coming down through the center and the center of the eyes coming through halfway down from there. The nose goes halfway between the eyes and the chin. Then put in the mouth above, halfway between the nose and the chin.

The question that I'm probably asked the most is "How do you paint black skin tones, and do you use black?" The answer to the first question is you paint black skin color just like any other skin, but you use different skin tones. The answer to the second question is "No." You don't use black in black skin — or in any other skin, for that matter. So, continue with our egg structure, now.

Put in the ear line, and the nose, then the mouth. Now squint, and get the eye shading in. Get the shadow on the side of the face very softly. With the canson paper, you see that it lays on just a little differently than on the velour. Visualize the hair coming through. You can place it coming way down below the chin line on the side, so give yourself plenty of room. Now bring it down over the forehead, with a bit more detail. We're using the dark sanguine, as always, for the beginning structure.

Now squint, and establish the chin line a little better. Now for the eyes, which are big and beautiful. Make them round, with an indication of the pupil and iris, and keep both eyes the same size. Indicate the eyebrows now. And remember, the ear is placed on the lines of the eyes and nose. Now for an indication of an earring.

And, of course, we have an earring that shows on the other side, too. Both earrings have to fall in line with each other.

II. HIGHLIGHTING

Start with the gold ochre #234,7 for the light and lay it in. Squint. Look for the lights, not just the extreme highlights, but also the lights that appear to help model the portrait.

We have a nice highlight on one side, and don't forget the neckline. Now, on the canson paper, sort of pull things together with your finger, so that it works itself into the surface of the paper. It's better to do this in the beginning stages, because it gives you something to build the color on.

III. THE FLESH TONES

Now, add some of the light sanguine color as usual, and lay it on to get some color into her flesh tones. Take the burnt sienna #411,5 (it's kind of a brick red, instead of a bright red), and use it to help build up the deeper colors to start. Lay it in quickly down under the chin, and up the side. All right, lay in again by smudging, getting it into the paper so it fills up a bit. Now a little warmth on the lips with the red color #371,5.

Now we'll take the dark blue/grey #727,3, and apply it into the shadows. Use it around the eyes as well, to build up the depth. Both sides have to match up with the eyes. Otherwise, you get them off-center. Indicate the eyebrows, the side of the cheek, and underneath the lip and under the jaw.

Take the dark sanguine and put it into the lips. Use some of the red color now in between the dark blue and the light to get added color in the transition from shadow to light. She's looking pretty red right now, but this is to get the warmth of

flesh color underneath.

Now, when you add some greenish tones #620,7 over the reds, see how it changes? There, pull it together a little bit. Don't smudge as much as you did earlier, and leave as much texture as you can.

IV. DETAILING

With the same lighter green, not real light but kind of an in-between olive green, see what happens when we apply it to those lighter flesh tones. We start to get a nice hue.

Now take the dark sanguine and use it now through the eyes, and through the shadows a bit. Now use #538,3 on the extreme shadow areas in the flesh tones to give it even more depth. And apply it even in the corner of the mouth where it can be accented. Then down the side of the face and under the jaw. This is a mars violet color, very dark, for the dark shadows.

V. EYES

We need to do something with the eyes. Use a grey/blue tone for the eyeball, up under where the upper lid comes over. Then a lighter grey/blue for the eyeball, then the black at this point, up under the lid to get the depth into the eyes.

We could add a few lashes here to the eyes to give them a little more added depth.

While we're at it, this would be a good time to put in some hair color. A dark blue first would be helpful to establish the hair, and basically lay in mass. Squint. Get something on there to make it work better. Because that's what you have to do with this paper — get it on and then subsequent colors will go on easier.

So there is the blue/grey tone, and now, with the black, add more body. Again, squint, and watch for the shadow side of the hair. Your deepest tones are here, and you can indicate this beautiful hair style with just a few strokes. Add some blue #640,7 and green #620,5, to the lights of the hair for more color.

Indicate the hair on the forehead. Put in some of the curls, waves, and the like. We can also indicate the shawl coming in now.

Okay, the eyes once more. We want to get some light in them. So start with your pale yellow, and work it into the eyeball with the bluish grey tone under it. Make sure you get the eye big enough. I'm going to add a little warmth with the sanguine color into the eye's iris—just a little brownish warmth to give it a little more color than just dead black.

Now, some white will help to put in the light. Place it carefully, adding a little highlight here and there.

VI. HIGHLIGHT DETAILS
Now, of course, we have to put our lights in. Shape the lips a little bit first, though, to get depth through the center.

Now use your light blue/grey #727,7 for some highlights. There is the shine on the nose. Put in blue lights in all the areas where you have your light tones. See the different type of texture we get with the canson paper? It gives an effect you can't get with velour, and it's an interesting change for you.

Now a nice pale green color should go in. This is all in the flesh tone—that's right, in the flesh. Remember how much more green is in the skin than most people realize. That goes for black skin, too.

Now for a nice tone to assist the lip color. Use the pink tone #546,8 here for the light. Remember the lower lip is lighter than the upper lip because it's catching the light. So squint your eyes, and put in

a popping highlight on the lower lip.

Let's add a little more depth of color around the eyes. Around the nostril add a little more color with the dark sanguine color—possibly a little more around the lips to accentuate them, too.

Now pull the hair down over the face, now that you have your lights in. It gives a better look, all the way around. Possibly a little more black would also help.

Take a look at your painting. And you have black skin without using black pigment.

VII. FINISHING TOUCHES
Remember to look for and try to see all the colors in whatever part of the portrait you're working on. You'll probably see colors you never imagined, all

coming together to create the image that artists see.

Now, the title of today's portrait is "Golden Earrings," so let's not forget them. Very quickly, take a gold ochre and indicate the earring. Then apply some orange #235,5 (which we haven't used very much) over that. Take a little olive green, some dark umber, and then some bright yellow and lay them in. Lastly, use some white to put in the earrings' highlights.

And that's that. You've completed "Golden Earrings."

This illustration shows the basic structure for this portrait.

"YOUNG MAN WITH A BEARD" 1981
26"x 20" canson paper
Rembrandt pastels

*Glasses and a beard are the two most challenging
characteristics of this portrait. Notice I said
"challenging," not "difficult," or "impossible." To me,
the idea of painting a portrait without the glasses,
then asking the model to put them on so I can paint
them, is as absurd as telling this portrait's model to
remove his beard for the same reason. After all, his
glasses are a natural part of his look—as is his
beard. Avoiding that "pasted-on" look is what
you'll learn while completing this painting.*

"YOUNG MAN WITH A BEARD"

I. STRUCTURING THE BASIC SHAPE

First of all, let's lay in the basic egg shape. You can see the structuring here on the canson paper, with the string wrapped around the egg, coming through the back, with his chin jutting out a bit. The eyes half way down the egg shape. The nose halfway between the eyes and chin, and the mouth is above halfway from the nose to the chin. Of course, the moustache takes over most of the upper lip area. Therefore, just indicate that with the under lip, and indicate, also, the shadows.

The ears fall in line with the nose and eyes. Make sure you get the ear back far enough, and there we have our basic structure. So let's start our portrait.

Now squint. See the shape of the shadows against the shape of the light.

The moustache takes in quite a bit of the mouth area; and the lower lip is still there, standing out. Indicate the shape of the black beard coming through now. Lay in your shadows. It's a little different with the beard, but the basics are still the same. One of the reasons I insist on having the glasses on while we do the portrait is that it looks more natural, as you will see.

Start detailing just a little. Get the nostrils set in position, as well as the thickness of the moustache. Note the width of the mouth underneath. Check all these points when you are doing your initial lay-in.

Now for a little triangle of beard—shape it up a little. Now put the glasses in. First, it might be better to establish the eyes though. They have to be in their natural position. Indicate the glasses above and below the eyes. When you're doing glasses, make sure you make them large enough so that they sit properly on the face. And make sure both sides of the glasses are the same size in proportion.

Now the line of the ear. Well, give him the beard first, and the ear sits in behind that, on the line of the nose and the eye. Indicate some hair coming from behind his neck. His neck comes in a little higher here.

Indicate the shirt, just a suggestion to show that there's a jacket over the top of it. And now it's time for some color.

II. HIGHLIGHTING

As usual, we'll start with the pale yellow. Blend it in, while squinting, looking for just the light areas against the dark, just as we looked a while ago for the dark areas against the light. Don't worry if it's coarse, because, with the canson paper, you do blend with the finger at first.

Now lay in some light on the lower lip. Under the lip, make sure to get enough tone going right into the beard, so you have enough flesh tone to build your hair on.

Don't forget the neck. Put some flesh tones under the beard, too. Lay some light sanguine over this now. See how that pops out? Lightly apply the sanguine, pull it together and you will get flesh tones.

Now go to the dark blue/grey #727,3 and lay in the shadows. We have quite a bit of shadow here, in the eyes, of course, and the eyelash that's underneath. Pull it together with your finger a bit. Indicate the nostrils, and the shadow on the side of the face. Get some dark blue color into the beard area, so it will merge with the flesh tones. We want to have the beard and glasses become an integral part of the portrait. So get it all in there together.

Now for some hair. Indicate a sharp line against the forehead, in the shadow, and pull the hair down over the face.

Make it come together, then lose it into the side of the flesh tones. It's a good idea to get this dark on right here because, as you'll notice, the flesh tone looks rather pale.

III. THE FLESH TONES

Now take your red color #371,5, and lay it on, creating not only soft warmth, but a little shadow, too. Now, a little more of the red to bring out some even stronger flesh color. Squint. Compare the value of color in here with the value of his shirt. See how much richer the flesh tone is than the shirt? So, you need color in there.

Take your gold ochre #234,7 now. I've told you before that, when painting with pastels, you blend your colors on the paper, rather than on a palette. This is what we'll do now.

You see, with the combination of the gold ochre and the red, you get a more natural flesh tone. Now, take the dark sanguine, and establish some shadows and the in-between tones. Indicate the shape of the glasses. Don't lose track of them. And the secret is: use just an indication.

IV. DETAILING

Now it's time for some greenish tones. Use olive green #620,7, and apply it to the shadows. You can see what those soft greenish tones do in there. Next, use a lighter green and apply it a little bit on the side. That helps make the portrait turn. Now under the nose, making it turn under. On the neck, as you're getting away from the light, there's a cooler tone.

V. EYES (and more detailing)

Now the eyes. First add a little bit of a bluish cast to the eyeball, a lighter blue cast into the eyeball. Then, with your black, apply color up under the lid, and into the eyes themselves.

Remember, avoid using

black for your flesh tones, just as you should avoid using white for them. Neither is a true color — they are used for tone. So use something other than black or white in your lights and darks.

We can, however, add black in the hair. His hair isn't all black — it has a little brownish tone, too. But where the depth shows, it appears to be black. Indicate the moustache. Pull the shadow side together. There.

Get the shape of the beard now. It's dark, back in behind the ear. If it's too harsh in there, squint your eyes and see what you can do about softening it up.

Use a little bit of dark sanguine and soften it into the hairline, so it doesn't leave a harsh edge. For more strength in the shadows, take the dark mars violet #538,3 and put it in some of the shadows for extra depth. Some can also go into the hairline, because his hair is brown in these areas. While we're at it, mix in a little gold ochre, too. If it's too dark, pull a little olive green across it.

Now let's put in some lights.

VI. HIGHLIGHT DETAILS
On the forehead there is a shadow cast from the hair, and the light coming over, is a greenish cast. It gives a nice color, doesn't it? Put a bright highlight on his nose, and a little on the cheek area. The lower lip can be a little cleaner and lighter. In the lips, just kind of get your pale yellow highlight in there and, very quickly, add a bit of that warm tone.

Put some light on the shadow side, to bring out the shape around the eye lids. We may as well put the light in his eye, too. Now we can establish the glasses. Put in mars violet #538,3. Shape them now. They get lighter as they come down. Now a touch of black, and we can suggest the eyebrows underneath.

Now let's get some light into the glasses to sparkle them up. Squint your eyes to see where the light really is. The highlights show the thickness of the glasses.

The ear should be a little lighter, as should portions of his neck. Indicate, again, his jacket. Then the neckline, and the shading on the collar. Now give him a white shirt. Leave the collar open, nice and loose. We can clean it up a little bit, and possibly put a little more gold in the hair, and even in the beard.

VII. FINISHING TOUCHES
You see, it really isn't difficult with a few basic techniques. The beard and glasses have become an integral part of the model's features. Plus, they were established along with the

natural development of the portrait. But there's one thing missing, something that will give a natural look to the glasses.

With your dark sanguine, put in the shadow of the glasses to make them sit down on his face. See the difference?

They say that one picture is worth a thousand words. Well, that may be, but I say that one skillfully applied shadow can save a thousand strokes.

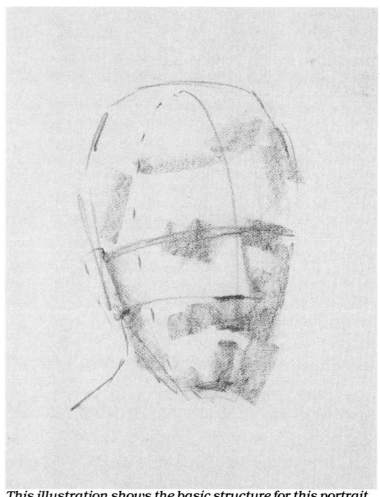

This illustration shows the basic structure for this portrait.

"LEILANI"   ***1981***

26"x 20" velour paper
Rembrandt pastels

*Aloha. This beautifully expressive Hawaiian word
says so much. Hello, good-bye, and it's also a way
for Hawaiians to extend their love. It's so very
indicative of the lovely, happy Hawaiian people.
I've spent a lot of time in Hawaii, and in this
portrait, we're going to capture Hawaii's beauty in
our painting called "Leilani." Leilani in English
means "flower of heaven." Our painting will
illustrate the smile and Hibiscus flower so typical
of the islands. The colors of Hawaii, you'll see, are
well-suited for our use of pastel.*

"LEILANI"

I. STRUCTURING THE BASIC SHAPE

As always, lay down your basic egg shape. The string wraps around to show the center line of her face. The eyes are halfway down from the top. Now, her head is tilted back slightly. Her chin is forward and, therefore, the line of her eyes is a little above center. The line will turn down slightly because it gives her that "upward" look. She has a happy smile.

Therefore, the mouth is pushed up a little more than normal. Okay, now the hairline comes over the egg, falling down over the eye. So lay in the eye shadow, and the nose pattern —just suggestions. Then the hibiscus, a big, voluptuous flower. Indicate the pattern of the hair. Then the beautiful neckline. You can see where that shoulder line comes. Now let's begin our portrait.

Squint, now, and lay shadows in the area where the eyes go, under the nose and, of course, the mouth. The mouth is raised at the corners. Indicate the open mouth and the teeth, too.

Outline her black hair against her flesh tones. Make the flower big, over-emphasize a little bit. We're featuring Hawaii, so make it stand out.

The neckline — again, bring your imaginary line along the shoulder line and see where that shoulder falls. Then indicate the shadow coming in to set off her face. Now indicate the volume of hair that just falls right out of the painting.

Start with the drawing of the mouth just a little. Keep the corners up. The teeth come down with the lip wrapped around them, along with the indication of that lower lip. There, now the smile starts.

Remember, the cheeks will have a little puffiness because of the smile. Work up into the eye area a little. Put in the shadow. And show the laugh lines, too. Now indicate the eyebrows. Now you can see how the smile starts to come when you add the high cheek, and don't forget the hair that comes in behind her head.

II. HIGHLIGHTING

Let's get the color started. Use your pale yellow #227,9 indicating the lower lid, and the cheek. Squint, now, and it becomes easy for you to see. Learn to see by simplifying that way. Use a simple highlight to indicate teeth. You can see how, even though it's just a highlight through there, the teeth have already begun to look like teeth. Put some light all over the facial area. And use some to indicate the hibiscus. Remember what I said about hair merging with the flesh. Parts of the flower merge with the flesh, so let it run through there.

Now the neckline, the clavicle, which is part of your anatomy lesson. Any time you're really interested in pursuing your portrait career, bone up on your anatomy. Pardon the pun, but it makes it easier to work, don't you agree?

III. THE FLESH TONES

Now take the light sanguine and just lay it all over the flesh tone. Over the teeth, everything, and make it a little stronger because she has very strong coppery color skin. Put on a little red #371,5, across the face and nose. This is a very warm area. The mouth, of course, is also very warm. In fact, we'll use the darker red on the lips when we finish them up.

At this point, put in a dark blue for the shadows, to indicate the depth. Put just a touch in the corner of the mouth. The mouth is usually quite warm and soft, so don't use too much. Under the chin, there's quite a strong shadow. Let's fill her chin out, as well as the jaw line.

You can indicate the hair now a little. Put the hair in, again, with the dark blue/grey. Notice I'm using the heel of the pastel along the line of the face. Use the heel, and spread it away from you, making a sharp edge. By using different pressures on the tip and heel of your stick, you gain much more latitude with your colors.

IV. DETAILING

Keep in mind the general shape of everything. The hibiscus is big, remember. Start with your lavender pink color #546,8 for the hibiscus. Use other colors to blend it, also. Use the lighter rose pink #362,9. That's a little pale. So go back to the deep red #318,5 for the center, and indicate the stamen. Blush it over the colors to indicate more of the reddish color of the hibiscus. While we're at it, let's put some of this red on her lips. Stretch those lips around the teeth, as well.

Now for some light. Add warm colors, indicative of her heritage. Now let's darken the hair. This is black. Again, use the heel of the pastel. Show the volume of the hair — but don't show every strand. Now there isn't just blue and black in the hair; there are other colors. So show a little ochre and green. See? It brings out the feeling we're after. We also need some of this gold ochre on the flesh tones where we have the red. Blushed lightly over the red, it gives you a golden color, especially as you come down away from the face, and onto the neck and shoulders.

Squint your eyes, now, and see how warm her face is. It's coming alive.

V. EYES

Take your black, so we can indicate the eyes. The upper lid is casting a shadow on the eyes, and on the eyeball. So show that and indicate the pupil, and the iris, in depth on your paper.

Now the eyes need more color. Let's use the dark sanguine. Where I've indicated with the dark blue, add the sanguine, to finish off the depth we need. Now a little darker at the corners of the eyes, blending it in there.

Underneath the lower lip, there's a little bit of a darker area. And, where the chin merges into the neck, soften that away so it blends in. There, that should be very nice.

VI. HIGHLIGHT DETAILS
Now let's go back to our light yellow for some more highlights. Use just enough to bring out some lights and to give the contour of her features. There's some beautiful highlight on the nose and the cheek, creating more of the smile. Over the upper lip, there's a little catch light you can achieve with the heel of your pastel. Now work on the upper lids, to make them come out and around.

The lower lid catches the light. This light you can softly merge up into the eyeball to give the roundness effect. Let's put a little warmth into her eyes with more dark sanguine, because her eyes aren't all black. They have a little warmth in there with the black.

Squint your eyes and carry through with the highlights. A little on the mouth and teeth, for example. Note that the teeth already have warmth to them. Take a little grey/blue and, very gently, run it through the teeth. Add some of the blue into the eyeball, also. Around the eye, sometimes we use greens, like you see in the portrait, for make-up and shadows.

Now, indicate the teeth again. Don't draw every tooth, but just indicate, with highlights. Mostly concentrate on the big smile, and the liquid appearance of the lips. Put a little light on the chin. Remember, too, that as you come down the face, the light is less intense. Your pressure on the pastel will be less here, and even less down in the neckline.

VII. FINISHING TOUCHES
Well, we have to indicate some eyebrows, don't we? Don't use black—use the darker blue #727,3. Put a little bit under the eye for shadows. Use a little bit of white to get some sparkle into the eye because, with a smile like that, she has to have sparkle. Now let's get that highlight in the eye. Again, we're after an impression instead of an exact likeness. Use a little shadow to give the hibiscus petals a little more reality, and we're about ready to call it quits.

We've reached that magic moment, so look over your portrait and decide if it's finished. And if you're in doubt, remember what I always say: "Knowing when to stop is just as important as knowing where to start."

This illustration shows the basic structure for this portrait.

"THE BANKER"   1981

26"x 20" velour paper
Rembrandt pastels

In this portrait, you'll find that even the staid, conservative image of a banker (which is how most people conceive bankers to be), we can find a truly interesting character to portray. You don't necessarily have to reach for the conservative colors automatically. As an artist, you should train yourself to look beyond the surface image and see the character within. Many times, what you see will surprise you.

"THE BANKER"

I. STRUCTURING THE BASIC SHAPE

First, lay in your basic egg shape, with the center line going, as always, around the back. The center of the eyes should be in the center of the face. His head is tilted up a little and, therefore, the line of the eyes will tend to come down. Put the line of the nose, parallel to that. The mouth is above halfway between the nose and the chin.

Now squint your eyes and check out that mass shadow area. Lay in the nose. Now add the shoulder line. The basic structure of the portrait is important for two reasons. Establishing the shape and proportion of the subject, and gaining a starting point to build on. So let's start our portrait.

The hair on the side comes out nice and full. With the back edge of the pastel, you can get a nice hard edge. The neckline comes down behind the jaw area and, the neck is a cylinder, so it's shaded on one side, and becomes lighter on the other.

The shoulder line is down a bit, as his chin is held proudly up. Follow through with the line of the other shoulder. See that it comes right through the mouth and carries on. He's looking like a banker already.

Now indicate the conservative jacket, shirt, and tie. The chin line is next and, of course, the upper lip — kind of hidden with the nice, trimmed moustache. Add a slight shadow under the lower lip.

Lay in a slight indication of the glasses, now. Remember the glasses are the same kind of problem as a hat, or a flower in the hair. Over-emphasize the dimensions a bit, or they'll appear too small. Whatever shadows are created with glasses can also be put on as you progress. And remember, the drawing aspect of your portrait is very important. Use your whole arm when you're working. Don't just use your fingers — get you're whole body into it.

II. HIGHLIGHTING

There's a highlight on his forehead, a nice bright light that shows up well. Use the back edge of your pale yellow pastel to lay in these initial lights, creating and modeling along with the light. Don't worry about the glasses being there. Go ahead and put your light on the cheek, and let it run right through and continue all the way down the face.

Now, let the highlight on the lower lip merge into the flesh tones on the light side of the face. Put some highlights in the neck, and you should be ready to add some warmth.

III. THE FLESH TONES

Take the light sanguine color and lay it on now. His complexion is not very dark, you'll notice. So don't apply your pastel as heavy as you might with someone whose complexion is very dark. Put it on all over, and run it into the hairline all the way, so you can bring the hair down and over it.

Now apply a bit of the red tone #371,5 very subtley. By the way, constantly wipe your pastels off to keep them fresh and clean when you're working with them. They tend to get dirty when you handle them too much, and when they rub color against color all the time.

Now add a little warmth with the red, especially into the lips. Lay in some around the eyes for warmth. Don't fuss with it, just get it on there. Then take the dark blue/grey pastel #727,3 for the shadows again. Lay them in, but get soft and subtle as you move down. You can also use this same color for the indication of the moustache. Add some shadow under the jawline, where it's strong.

Squint. See the simplicity in the shadows, and in the light. Lay in some shadow along the side of the face. His hair is quite grey, as befitting a banker, I suppose, so apply some color to the shadow. Check along the side of the hairline, and let it merge with the flesh tones. At the same time, we can show the tie, which needs only to be an indication of his dress, his stature, and so on. Indicate the conservatism of our portrait.

IV. DETAILING

Now lay the darker sanguine in, to kind of refine the shadows a little over the blue cast that we have. This will bring a little more color into the shadow. You can use this also on the lips and in the shadow area. Soften the edge of the nose. Look at his nose closely. There are shadows, and there are lights. In between that shadow and light, there's a transition of warmth. Keep this in mind whenever you merge colors between the light and the dark.

Let's indicate the glasses now, just slightly. Keep them in line, naturally. And we'd better get some lights in there, too. Now put a little red onto his shirt. By using red, and going over it with a soft pink, we'll arrive at our color. That's the idea of pastels — you're painting on your paper, not mixing on your palette.

Now add some highlight to the forehead. His complexion not being very dark, we use a little more highlight to brush over everything and make it just a little softer. There's a nice light on his nose. On the shadow side, your lights are not as intense as they are on the side where the lighting is coming from. Squint and look at your subject as a whole, and check the values I'm telling you about.

V. EYES

Now add a little twinkle in his eye. By adding a little bit of light, and turning his mouth up a bit, you can see the smile emerge. Now add some more depth in the eyes, up under the upper lid again, very dark. Put in the iris and the pupils.

Use a little black on his moustache, but very softly, because it's a little bit grey there, too. Get some depth along in there with the black. Now the grey hair is, of course, not just black and white. Use a little blue to start building up the grey instead of just coming in with pure white. Now use the white to run over that and bring out the light tones, giving him that distinguished look. He has a touch of grey where the moustache is, so add it.

While we have the white, let's finish up in the eyes. They have a little more color than just black in the pupil. The iris has kind of an ochre tone, so use your dark greenish ochre and a little bit of the gold ochre. Add a little light into the iris, and then with the white, sparkle up the eyes.

We have to show the glasses but, also, there's a beautiful shadow created from the glasses on his flesh. So let those shadows follow the contour of his face, just kind of disappearing into the shadow. Now put in the glass itself. For the rim, use your umber color #408,5. Don't put them in hard all the way around. Just put them in here and there, to indicate. Keep them sketchy, and let them go back in under the hair.

Now, of course, we have to show that they're glasses. So lay in a real bright highlight. Squint your eyes. It lets you see those lights a little easier.

VI. HIGHLIGHT DETAILS
Now, for some of those other lights in the glasses use the gold ochre #234,7. You can also put in a little white where it's needed. Opposite from the light source, remember. And that's about all you need for the indication of the glasses.

We can add some more hair. Remember what I've said about hair: put in the volume first. Forget about every little strand. On the shadow side, go a little softer with white, not quite so intense, although there's a nice light we can see.

Add some more definition to the nostril. Look it over again. Increase the shadow. It should be more intense where it touches the glasses.

We need some cool tones now, so let's get the reflected light with our green tone #620,7. Be careful of reflected lights. Don't get them too strong. Again, squint. See the reflected lights fall back into the shadow, and aren't as brilliant as you might think. Put in a little softness of green around the side to create the illusion of the contour of his face turning away from you. And just a little greenish tone under the nose to turn it slightly under.

And I think we're nearing the end of yet another portrait.

VII. FINISHING TOUCHES
Now add a little more strength in the mouth. Also, put in a little shadow down in his shirt to make it look more believable. Add a bit of depth to the tie. And don't forget the shadow on the neck. There, you're about finished.

Look over your portrait. Have you captured that "banker image" to your satisfaction? Good. You've just completed another portrait, and finished your first study of a model who turned out to be rather exciting in spite of his "stuffy" image.

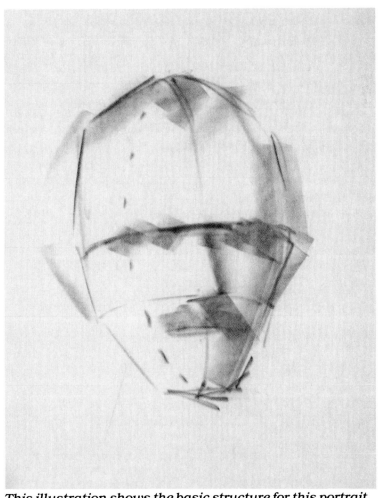

This illustration shows the basic structure for this portrait.

"GREEN EYES"   1981

26" x 20" velour paper
Rembrandt pastels

It has been said that the eyes are the windows of the soul. Movies have been made about them. Fortunes have been spent to enhance them. I personally feel that they give life to a portrait— any portrait. So in this portrait, we'll concentrate on the eyes as a focal point for the entire painting.

"GREEN EYES"

I. STRUCTURING THE BASIC SHAPE

With your sanguine, let's lay in the basic egg shape, as always. The string goes behind, wrapped right around the head. Now put in the line for the eyes, which gives her that direction in which she is looking. The nose is halfway from the eyes to the chin, the mouth above halfway. The most important thing, remember, is the eyes. With the light coming in as it is, there is the look of a heavy upper lid. It, in turn, casts a definite shadow on the "ball" that's in there. Look and you will see the contour there, underneath.

With the lower lid, you have this same feeling going around and into the shadow. Put the pupil in the center, and the iris around it. By deepening your stroke above and letting it fade down, you get the feeling created by the lashes and upper lid. Remember, the lower lid will be light.

Okay, let's begin the portrait.

In this portrait, we're going to enlarge the size of the face, and of the head a bit, so that the eyes will be prominent and a little more in evidence.

Remember that the eye lids are stretched over the eyeball, so you have to contour them up and around and over to achieve the effect we're after.

Keep the eyes in line, and don't forget the thickness of that upper lid which makes her eyes look so lovely. Squint, and simplify where you can. Lightly suggest the nose, then do the same with the mouth. And underneath the mouth, there's a little shadow. Indicate the shadow of her hair coming through and just sort of falling out. Then the chin, and the shadow that the chin creates on the neck. Suggest the hair, so you'll have an idea where everything will appear, remembering to keep the hair nice, loose, and soft.

All right, now for some highlights.

II. HIGHLIGHTING

Now punch in those highlights. First on the nose. Then the whole area, the cheek bones as well. As we've done before, squint, and suggest the light pattern. Lay some in on that beautiful lower lid. That helps to accentuate those eyes, which is what we're trying to do, after all.

The upper and lower lids catch the light. Don't forget the area above the lids to create the feeling of roundness and form around the eye itself. On the eyeball, you can create the suggestion of it merging out into the light from the dark. Don't worry about any more highlights now. In fact, without the subtle lights that give you your form, your highlights don't mean much. Your lower lights, then, are actually more important than your highlights. Keep that in mind.

III. THE FLESH TONES

Now just suggest the neck. And, again, using the light sanguine, lay in color over everything for her complexion. Keep it nice and fresh and loose. Add a little more color around the eyes, and around the lid. The eye is not just in the immediate area — it takes in all of the socket and everything surrounding it. We have to build the eye, and then cover the whole socket area.

We can also give her a little more warmth throughout the rest of her features. Add a little bit on the mouth and cheeks, still using the light sanguine color.

Now add a little more warmth with the red #371,5. Use some through the area of the eye, and a little bit on the cheek, but keep this part of the portrait subtle. Remember, the most important part of this whole portrait is the eyes.

With the blue/grey #727,3 over-emphasize the shadow that is cast above and below the eye socket on the shadow side. Now for the other eye. Remember, this eye is on the light side, so don't give it the same depth as the eye that's on the shadow side. Keep it a little cleaner.

We haven't even shown the color of her eyes yet, which are green (that's why we're calling her "Green Eyes"). But while we're at it with the dark blue, we can suggest again a little of the shadow in the hair. Cut the chin in a little bit, too. In fact, if you squint, you can lose that into the shadow.

IV. DETAILING

Work the whole portrait, as I've said in the past. But, we are concentrating on the eyes, so let's get back to them.

Take the dark sanguine to start building around the eyes and the lids, adding warmth and depth. Then we can put more light over it and model it, sort of like you do with clay. Those beautiful heavy upper lids really give an exotic appearance. Let's put some color into the eye now. Take your green #608,9, and lay in some color. It looks pretty bright, I know, but never be afraid of using color.

Now the white of the eye is, of course, not entirely white. There's a lot of color in the eye, so with a light blue/grey #727,9, put in the eyeball area. In fact, use this blue, rather than the green, in the surrounding flesh. We can also use some of the blue to give the feeling of shadow and shade on the eye itself.

Next, take your black and start to help the eye emerge a little better. Again, soften it away as you work it up under the upper lid, so it kind of comes out from the shadow into the light. And on the shadow side, make sure that you show it going into the shadow. Follow the portrait in the book as your visual reference.

V. SOME LIGHTS FOR THE EYES

Take the pale yellow #227,9 and put some of it in to bring out the lights on each side. Put some light towards the center where the light is hitting. The lower lid now must show some light. The lower lids have a light on them, which helps to add more contour to the rest of the facial features. Let's even add some of these lights back into the rest of the features, so that the whole portrait has some continuity to it.

Now use dark blue #727,3, not a black, for the eyebrows. Just suggest them, and let them blend in with the face. All right, take the black again into the eye, and work around the iris and pupil, bringing them out some more. Don't make the iris a round ball, but a kind of hex shape. When you add more shadow depth into it, you lose the upper part of the iris, now she's beginning to get those romantic eyes we're looking for.

Add some lashes at this point, but just a suggestion, again. Let it be a dark area. Do you see them now?

Let's do the same thing to the other eye. Again, just a suggestion. The green in the eyes could be a bit too raw, so let's put in some color. Use your sanguine, and softly lay in a little warmth, taking away the raw look. But keep them definitely green.

Add a light, on the light side, not the shadow side. The eyeball has to have some light on it, too, so take your pale yellow and softly work it into the eyeball to give it a more rounded feeling. Don't forget the depth under the eye, either, because she has those beautiful lower lashes for us to consider.

Use your dark blue/grey #727,3 to suggest the lower lashes. Now put a little bit of warmth into the corner of the eyes with your red, but don't put any on the eyeballs themselves— we don't want red eyes.

But you do want that little warmth in the corner. So use your white and add a little catch light there. And they're starting to get that liquid look, aren't they? In the corner, on top of the warmth, put some light in, again, always remembering where your light is coming from.

VI. HIGHLIGHT DETAILS

Now, for a more sensuous look, get that highlight up into the dark. Run through it to give it a glassy look.

Now that we have the eyes, we can develop the hair a little more. Use your umber color #408,5, and develop the hair softly, suggestively. Don't forget those nice bangs over there, either. Now let's put a little more color into the hair, using gold ochre #234,7. Suggest the volume, the body of the hair. That's better. Just show that it does come out and around, and add a little bit of light on the hair where it comes forward.

Can you see the green in it? You can if you squint your eyes. But there's also warmth, so let's take the dark sanguine, and bring back a little bit of warmth, so that it isn't getting too far away from the rest of the portrait.

Speaking of color, the brow needs some attention. Let's just indicate it with a light blue #727,7, and add a little darker blue for the shadow, to indicate the form. Again, be suggestive. Now add a little more light around the eyes, building up wherever you can.

Now work the flesh tone just a little bit more. Keep it loose. Suggest, rather than detail!

VII. FINISHING TOUCHES

Suggestion is something I've talked a lot about. It's so much more important to these portraits than going into labored detail. Suggestion serves the dual purpose of simplifying the facial features while, at the same time, giving full impact to the eyes. See how those eyes look right out of the portrait?

They're telling you, in a beautifully expressive way, that it's time to stop. That's always an important decision. But, once again (or do I have to tell you?) knowing when to stop is every bit as important as knowing where to start.

Congratulations. Those "Green Eyes" are gorgeous.

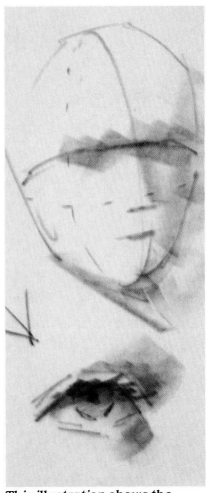

This illustration shows the basic structure for this portrait.

A FINAL WORD FROM THE ARTIST

*Well, now you've completed all 13 portraits.
And I hope you've learned a lot while doing them,
because it's always a pleasure to me to be able to
teach someone how to truly enjoy painting
a lovely picture.*

*The DeMille technique is, as I've said many
times, a very effective, powerful pastel application
that can result in portraits you can be proud of for
many years to come.*

*In closing, I want to stress, however, that
no technique by itself is a formula for success.
The only formula that I know to work is this:
practice, practice, practice. By constantly honing
your skills, and studying the techniques outlined
in **Portraits in Pastel**, you can become more
proficient than you realize. I hope you will continue
developing your skills with the pastels. I have been
happy with them for years, and shall be happy
with them for a lot more to come. Good luck.*

The Author

DETAILS AND DEMONSTRATIONS

"SUMMER SHADOWS"

Complete the imaginary line of the egg shape under the hat for your basic structure. Keep the hat big enough to cover her head. Now lay in the shadows as you see them.

Using your pale yellow #227,9, lay in the highlights as illustrated. Don't forget, the same color is used on the hat and the face.

Take your light sanguine and glaze it across all flesh tones to give you instant color. Use your red #371,5 to add additional warmth.

Now add the color to her dress and hat band. Keep it loose. Continue color enhancement by following the illustration.

Here you can see the additional color tones that are added before the finishing details of light and shadow.

Review your progress and compare it to the illustrations. Make sure you capture the lights on her face, cast by the holes in the hat.

"THE SEA CAPTAIN"

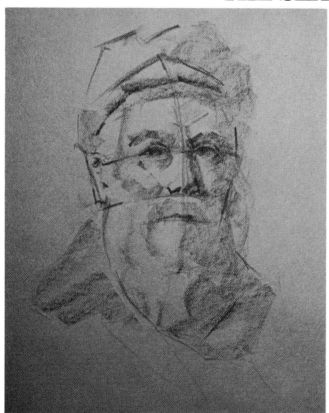

In this portrait, the problem of the beard and the hat covering the egg shape can be overcome simply by remembering the following: Visualize the basic egg shape under the hat and the beard and draw that imaginary line as in other portraits.

Copy this illustration completely before going to the next.

Keep the highlights simple. With your pale yellow, #227,9, lay in the highlights as they appear in this illustration.

Now lay in your light sanguine over all flesh tones. Because this is canson paper, lightly rub it in to pull the tones together.

Let's get some strength into the shadows by using your dark blue/grey #727,3. Now, add red #371,5 between shadows and light to add extra color. By adding gold ochre #234,7, you will achieve a truer flesh tone.

Now add your blue/grey #727,3 to the hat and clothing. To start the final detailing, add grey tones to the hair and beard. Complete the portrait by detailing the highlights and shadow. Always refer to the completed portrait for color direction.

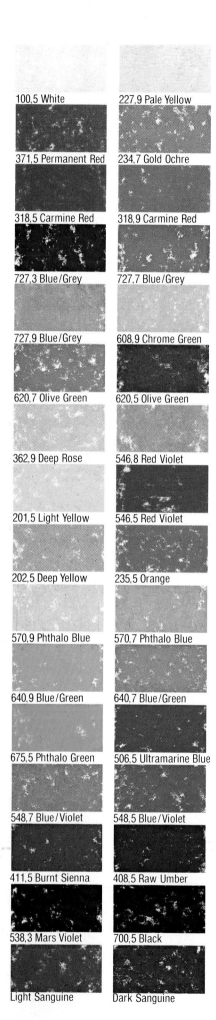

100,5 White

227,9 Pale Yellow

371,5 Permanent Red

234,7 Gold Ochre

318,5 Carmine Red

318,9 Carmine Red

727,3 Blue/Grey

727,7 Blue/Grey

727,9 Blue/Grey

608,9 Chrome Green

620,7 Olive Green

620,5 Olive Green

362,9 Deep Rose

546,8 Red Violet

201,5 Light Yellow

546,5 Red Violet

202,5 Deep Yellow

235,5 Orange

570,9 Phthalo Blue

570,7 Phthalo Blue

640,9 Blue/Green

640,7 Blue/Green

675,5 Phthalo Green

506,5 Ultramarine Blue

548,7 Blue/Violet

548,5 Blue/Violet

411,5 Burnt Sienna

408,5 Raw Umber

538,3 Mars Violet

700,5 Black

Light Sanguine

Dark Sanguine

ADDITIONAL MATERIALS AND COORDINATED COLOR CHART FOR "PORTRAITS IN PASTEL"

A special *PORTRAITS IN PASTEL* kit has been personally prepared by Leslie B. DeMille for this book as well as his television show. Information about obtaining this kit may be requested from:

Leslie B. DeMille
Post Office Box 2066
Costa Mesa, California 92626